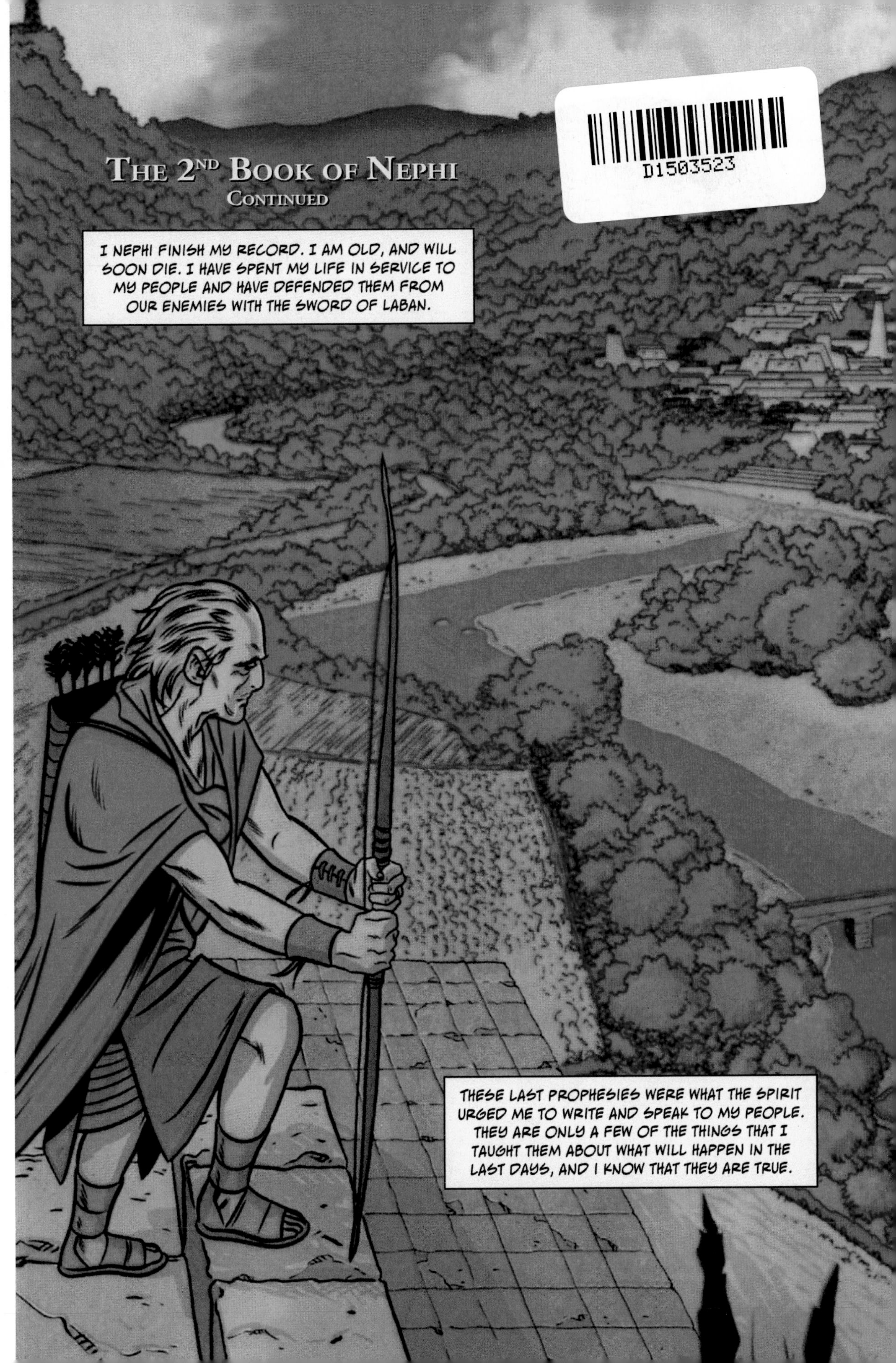
THE 2ND BOOK OF NEPHI
CONTINUED
I NEPHI FINISH MY RECORD. I AM OLD, AND WILL SOON DIE. I HAVE SPENT MY LIFE IN SERVICE TO MY PEOPLE AND HAVE DEFENDED THEM FROM OUR ENEMIES WITH THE SWORD OF LABAN.
THESE LAST PROPHESIES WERE WHAT THE SPIRIT URGED ME TO WRITE AND SPEAK TO MY PEOPLE. THEY ARE ONLY A FEW OF THE THINGS THAT I TAUGHT THEM ABOUT WHAT WILL HAPPEN IN THE LAST DAYS, AND I KNOW THAT THEY ARE TRUE.

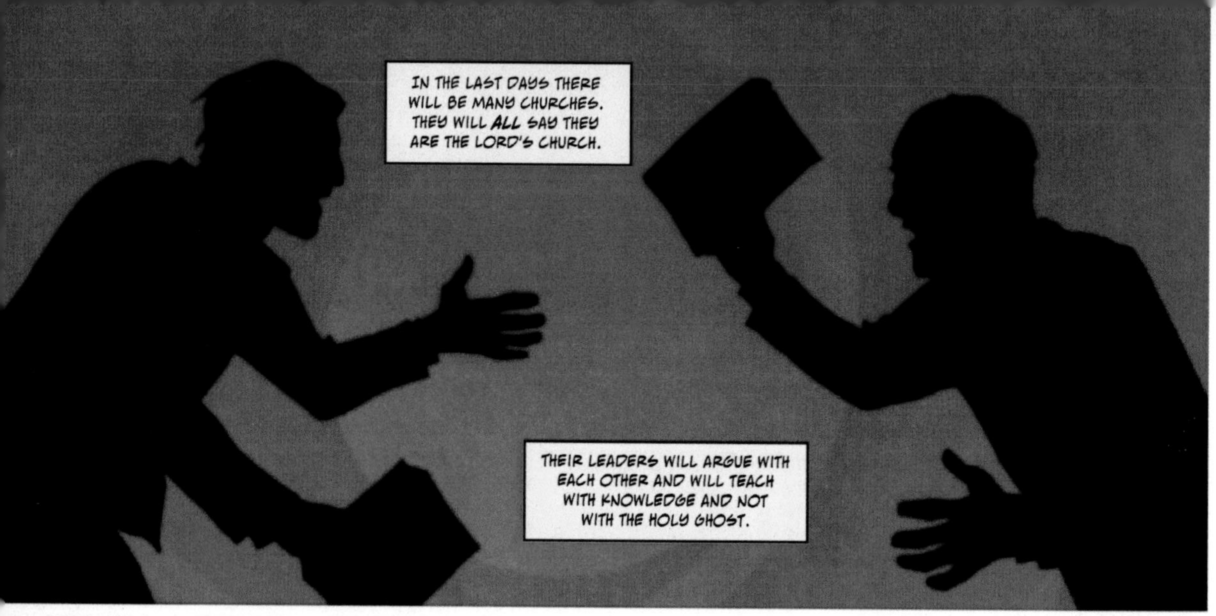
IN THE LAST DAYS THERE WILL BE MANY CHURCHES. THEY WILL ALL SAY THEY ARE THE LORD'S CHURCH.
THEIR LEADERS WILL ARGUE WITH EACH OTHER AND WILL TEACH WITH KNOWLEDGE AND NOT WITH THE HOLY GHOST.
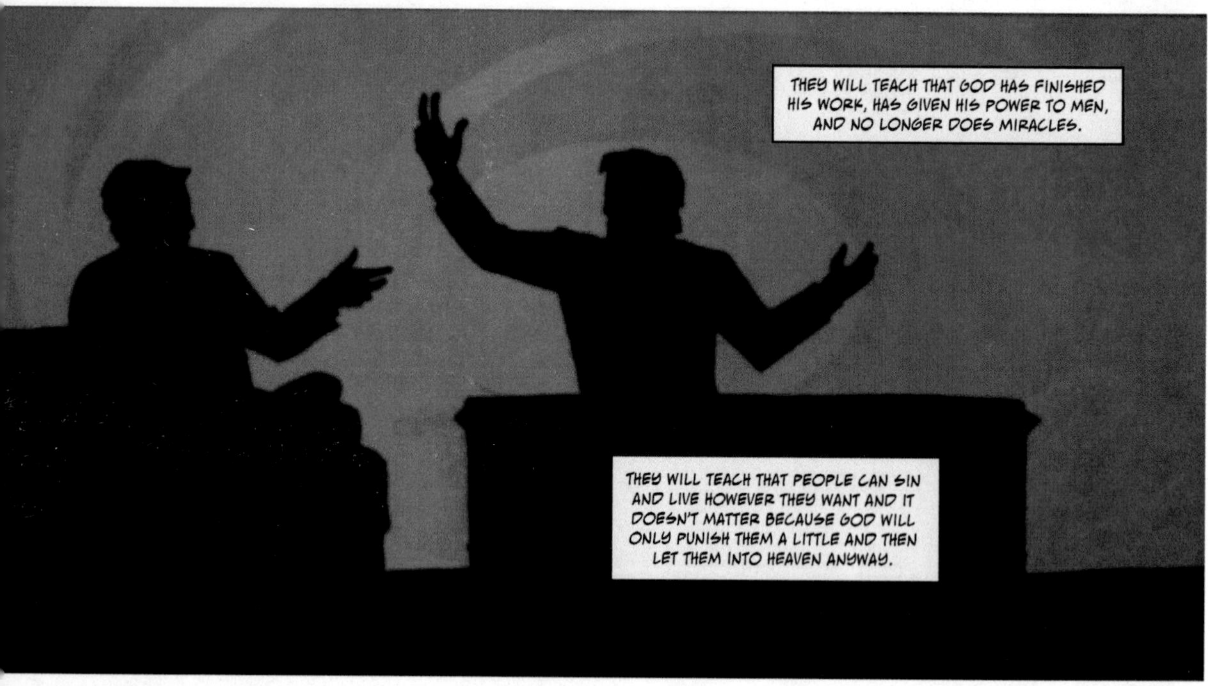
THEY WILL TEACH THAT GOD HAS FINISHED HIS WORK, HAS GIVEN HIS POWER TO MEN, AND NO LONGER DOES MIRACLES.
THEY WILL TEACH THAT PEOPLE CAN SIN AND LIVE HOWEVER THEY WANT AND IT DOESN'T MATTER BECAUSE GOD WILL ONLY PUNISH THEM A LITTLE AND THEN LET THEM INTO HEAVEN ANYWAY.
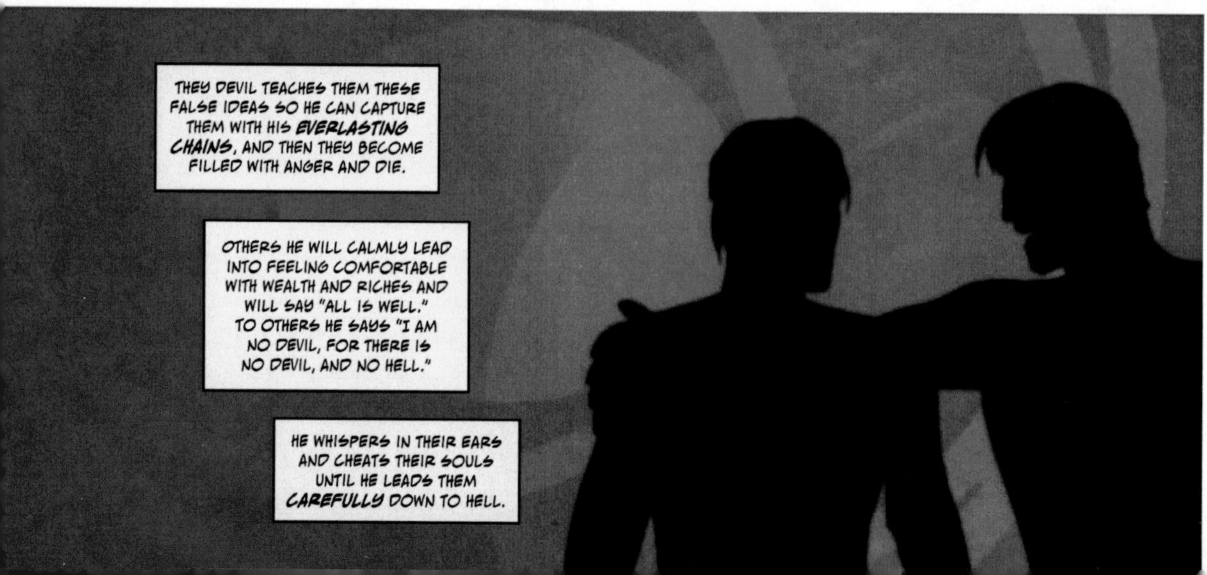
THEY DEVIL TEACHES THEM THESE FALSE IDEAS SO HE CAN CAPTURE THEM WITH HIS EVERLASTING CHAINS, AND THEN THEY BECOME FILLED WITH ANGER AND DIE.
OTHERS HE WILL CALMLY LEAD INTO FEELING COMFORTABLE WITH WEALTH AND RICHES AND WILL SAY "ALL IS WELL." TO OTHERS HE SAYS "I AM NO DEVIL, FOR THERE IS NO DEVIL, AND NO HELL."
HE WHISPERS IN THEIR EARS AND CHEATS THEIR SOULS UNTIL HE LEADS THEM CAREFULLY DOWN TO HELL.

The Golden Plates #5
Premium Edition: Nephi & Jacob's Teachings
& The Olive Tree Allegory

Drawings by: **Michael Allred**
Coloring by: **Laura Allred**
Adaptation by: **Michael Allred** & **Andrew Knaupp**
Lettering by: **Andrew Knaupp**

Copyright 2017 Michael Allred
All rights reserved

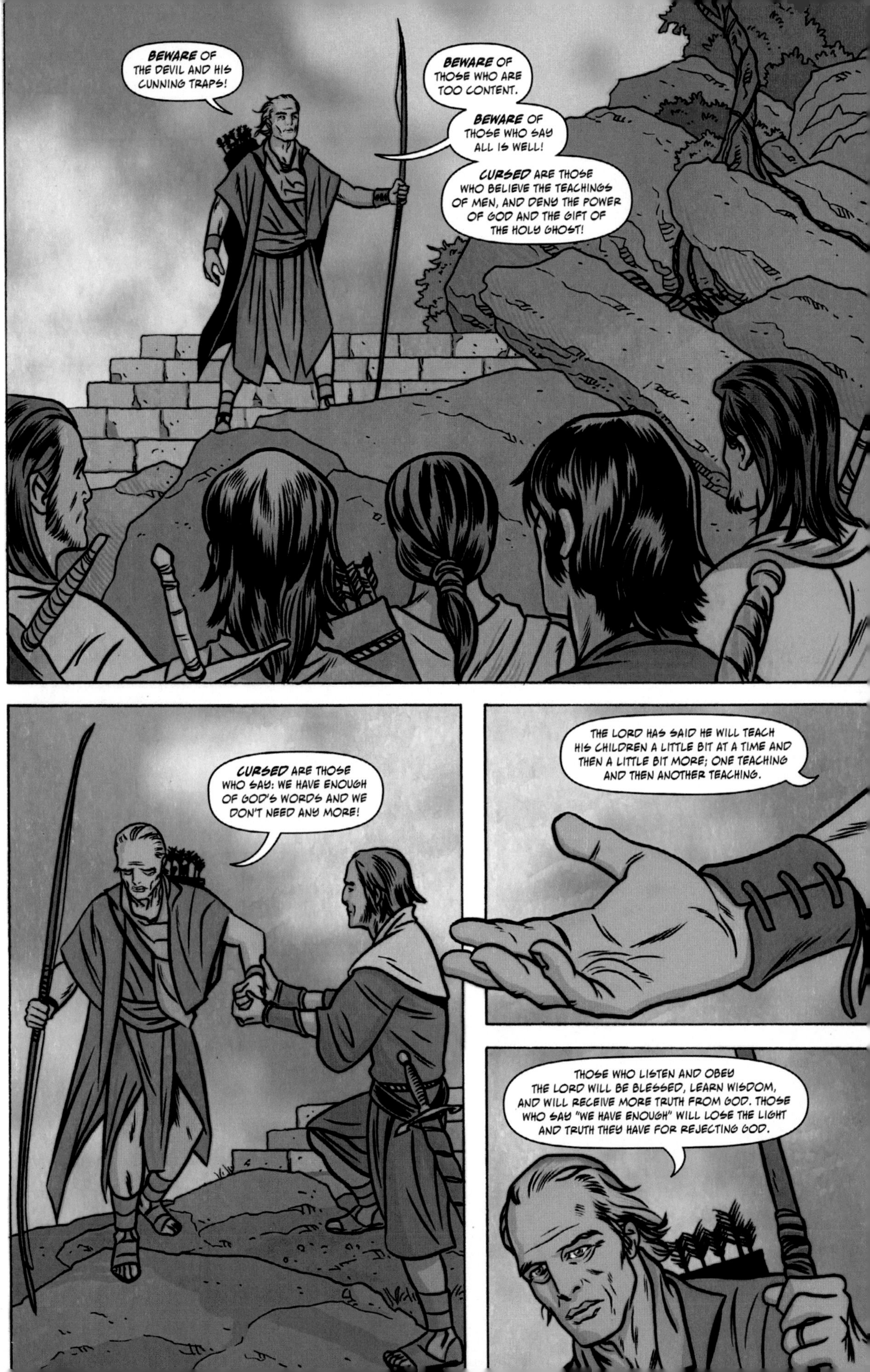
BEWARE OF THE DEVIL AND HIS CUNNING TRAPS!
BEWARE OF THOSE WHO ARE TOO CONTENT.
BEWARE OF THOSE WHO SAY ALL IS WELL!
CURSED ARE THOSE WHO BELIEVE THE TEACHINGS OF MEN, AND DENY THE POWER OF GOD AND THE GIFT OF THE HOLY GHOST!
CURSED ARE THOSE WHO SAY: WE HAVE ENOUGH OF GOD'S WORDS AND WE DON'T NEED ANY MORE!
THE LORD HAS SAID HE WILL TEACH HIS CHILDREN A LITTLE BIT AT A TIME AND THEN A LITTLE BIT MORE; ONE TEACHING AND THEN ANOTHER TEACHING.
THOSE WHO LISTEN AND OBEY THE LORD WILL BE BLESSED, LEARN WISDOM, AND WILL RECEIVE MORE TRUTH FROM GOD. THOSE WHO SAY "WE HAVE ENOUGH" WILL LOSE THE LIGHT AND TRUTH THEY HAVE FOR REJECTING GOD.

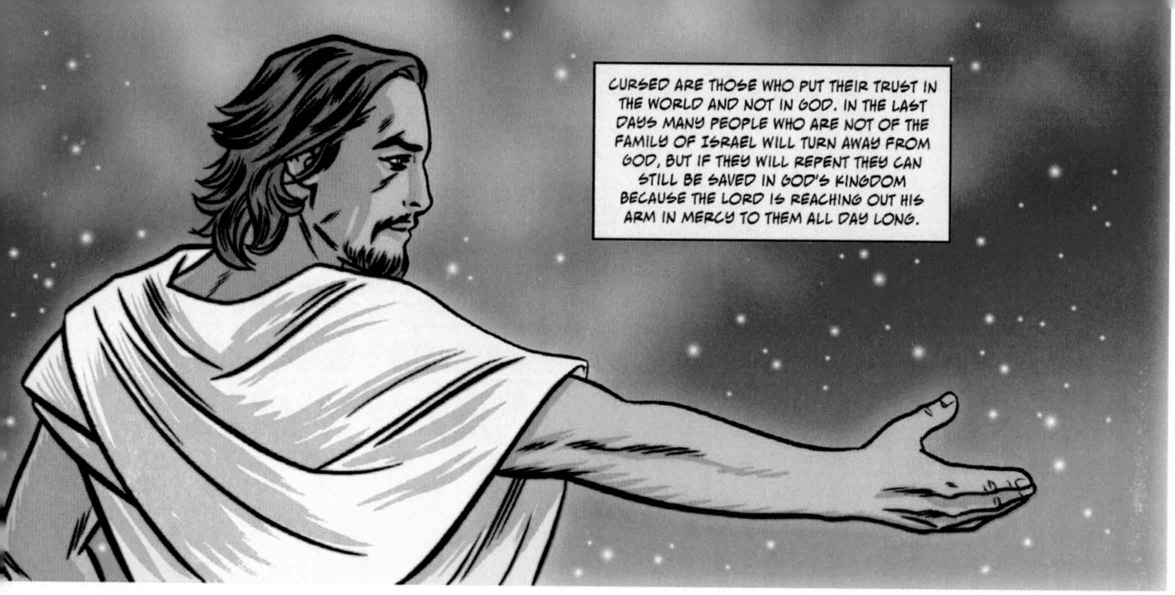
CURSED ARE THOSE WHO PUT THEIR TRUST IN THE WORLD AND NOT IN GOD. IN THE LAST DAYS MANY PEOPLE WHO ARE NOT OF THE FAMILY OF ISRAEL WILL TURN AWAY FROM GOD, BUT IF THEY WILL REPENT THEY CAN STILL BE SAVED IN GOD'S KINGDOM BECAUSE THE LORD IS REACHING OUT HIS ARM IN MERCY TO THEM ALL DAY LONG.

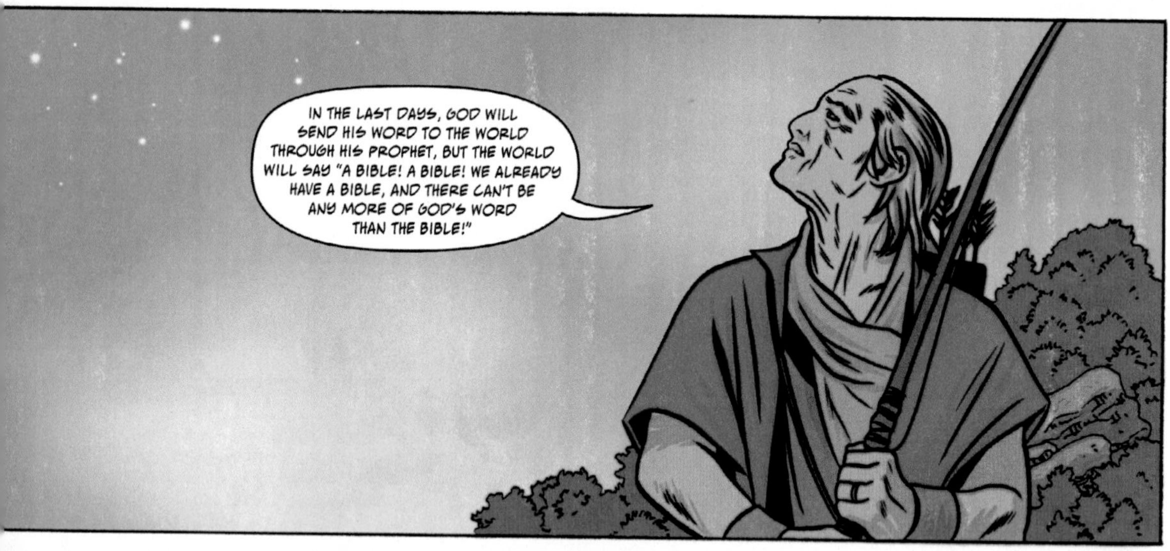
IN THE LAST DAYS, GOD WILL SEND HIS WORD TO THE WORLD THROUGH HIS PROPHET, BUT THE WORLD WILL SAY "A BIBLE! A BIBLE! WE ALREADY HAVE A BIBLE, AND THERE CAN'T BE ANY MORE OF GOD'S WORD THAN THE BIBLE!"

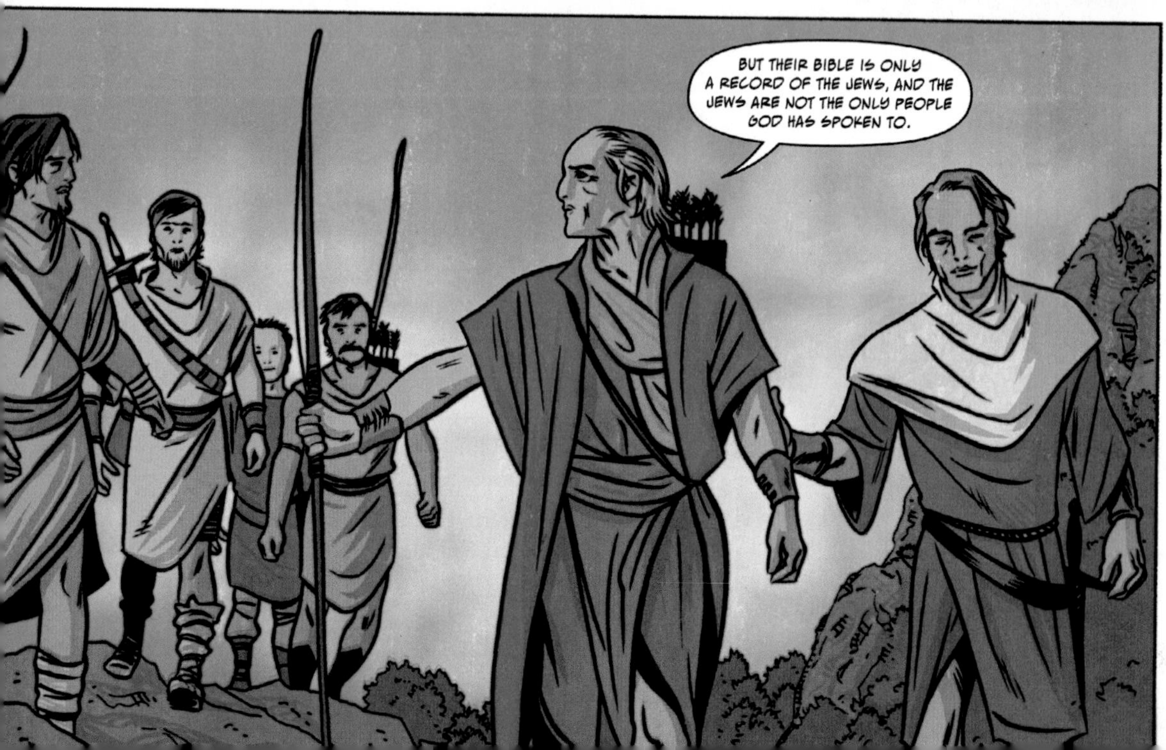
BUT THEIR BIBLE IS ONLY A RECORD OF THE JEWS, AND THE JEWS ARE NOT THE ONLY PEOPLE GOD HAS SPOKEN TO.

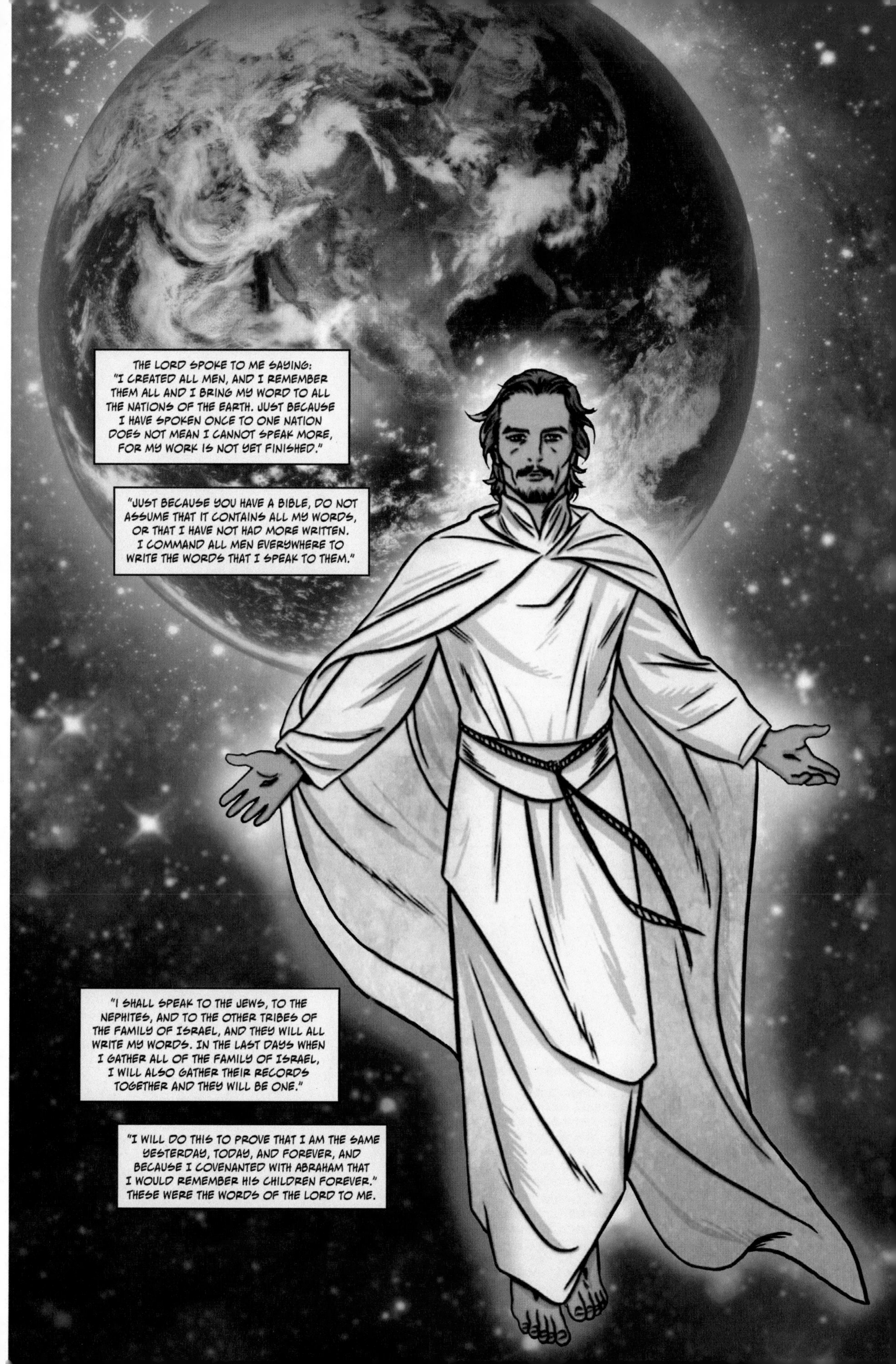
THE LORD SPOKE TO ME SAYING: "I CREATED ALL MEN, AND I REMEMBER THEM ALL AND I BRING MY WORD TO ALL THE NATIONS OF THE EARTH. JUST BECAUSE I HAVE SPOKEN ONCE TO ONE NATION DOES NOT MEAN I CANNOT SPEAK MORE, FOR MY WORK IS NOT YET FINISHED."
"JUST BECAUSE YOU HAVE A BIBLE, DO NOT ASSUME THAT IT CONTAINS ALL MY WORDS, OR THAT I HAVE NOT HAD MORE WRITTEN. I COMMAND ALL MEN EVERYWHERE TO WRITE THE WORDS THAT I SPEAK TO THEM."
"I SHALL SPEAK TO THE JEWS, TO THE NEPHITES, AND TO THE OTHER TRIBES OF THE FAMILY OF ISRAEL, AND THEY WILL ALL WRITE MY WORDS. IN THE LAST DAYS WHEN I GATHER ALL OF THE FAMILY OF ISRAEL, I WILL ALSO GATHER THEIR RECORDS TOGETHER AND THEY WILL BE ONE."
"I WILL DO THIS TO PROVE THAT I AM THE SAME YESTERDAY, TODAY, AND FOREVER, AND BECAUSE I COVENANTED WITH ABRAHAM THAT I WOULD REMEMBER HIS CHILDREN FOREVER." THESE WERE THE WORDS OF THE LORD TO ME.

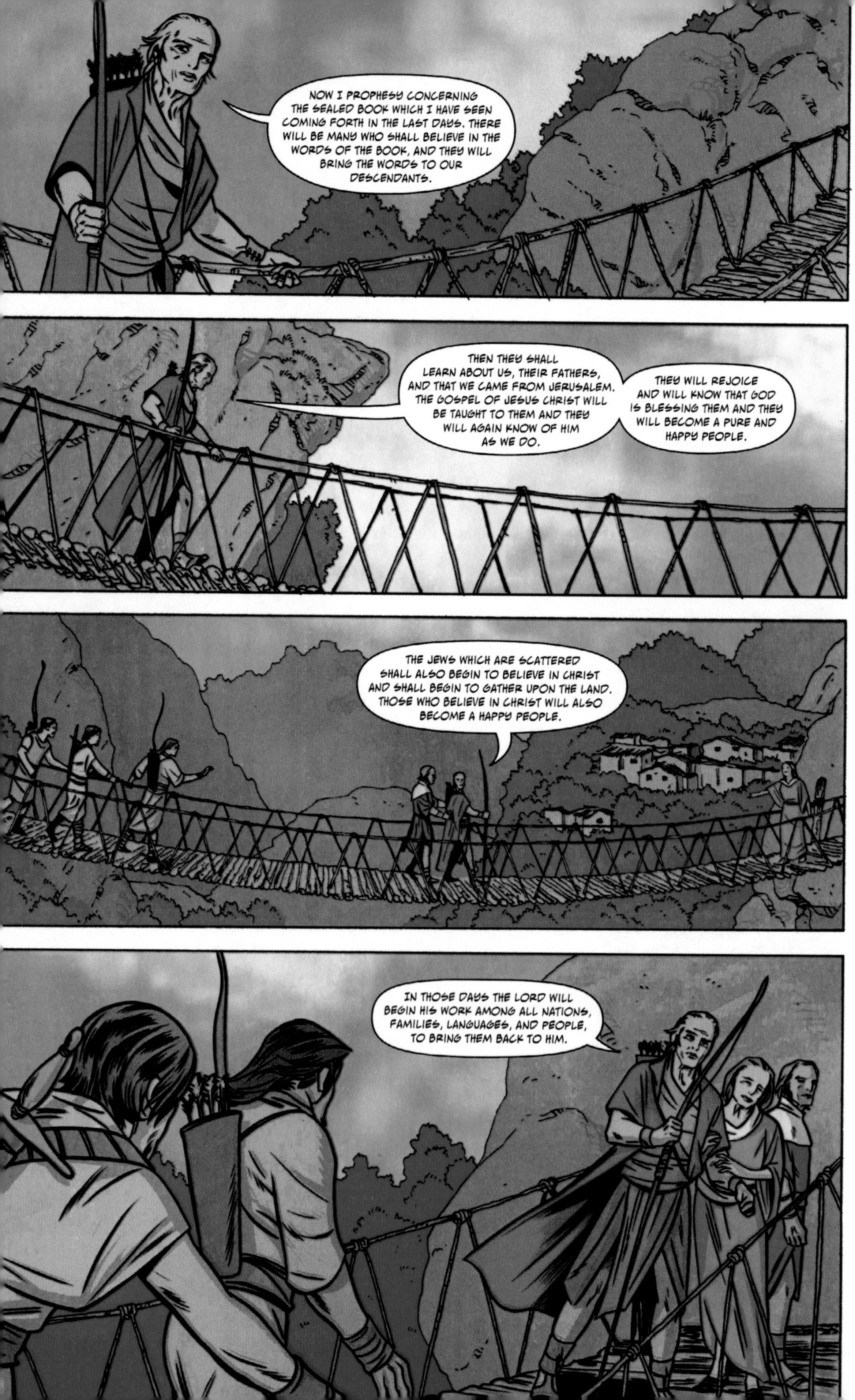
NOW I PROPHESY CONCERNING THE SEALED BOOK WHICH I HAVE SEEN COMING FORTH IN THE LAST DAYS. THERE WILL BE MANY WHO SHALL BELIEVE IN THE WORDS OF THE BOOK, AND THEY WILL BRING THE WORDS TO OUR DESCENDANTS.
THEN THEY SHALL LEARN ABOUT US, THEIR FATHERS, AND THAT WE CAME FROM JERUSALEM. THE GOSPEL OF JESUS CHRIST WILL BE TAUGHT TO THEM AND THEY WILL AGAIN KNOW OF HIM AS WE DO.
THEY WILL REJOICE AND WILL KNOW THAT GOD IS BLESSING THEM AND THEY WILL BECOME A PURE AND HAPPY PEOPLE.
THE JEWS WHICH ARE SCATTERED SHALL ALSO BEGIN TO BELIEVE IN CHRIST AND SHALL BEGIN TO GATHER UPON THE LAND. THOSE WHO BELIEVE IN CHRIST WILL ALSO BECOME A HAPPY PEOPLE.
IN THOSE DAYS THE LORD WILL BEGIN HIS WORK AMONG ALL NATIONS, FAMILIES, LANGUAGES, AND PEOPLE, TO BRING THEM BACK TO HIM.

I LOVE TO SPEAK PLAINLY, BECAUSE THAT IS HOW THE LORD WORKS. HE GIVES LIGHT AND UNDERSTANDING, AND SPEAKS TO PEOPLE IN THEIR OWN LANGUAGE AND IN A WAY THAT THEY WILL UNDERSTAND.

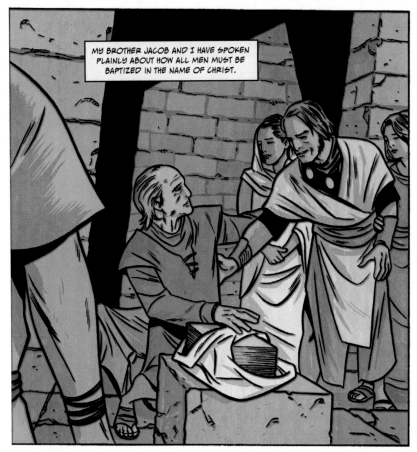

MY BROTHER JACOB AND I HAVE SPOKEN PLAINLY ABOUT HOW ALL MEN MUST BE BAPTIZED IN THE NAME OF CHRIST.

I HAVE SEEN THAT THE LORD HIMSELF WILL BE BAPTIZED.

IF JESUS CHRIST, WHO IS *SINLESS*, NEEDS TO BE BAPTIZED, THEN HOW MUCH MORE DO WE NEED TO BE BAPTIZED, *BEING SINFUL?*

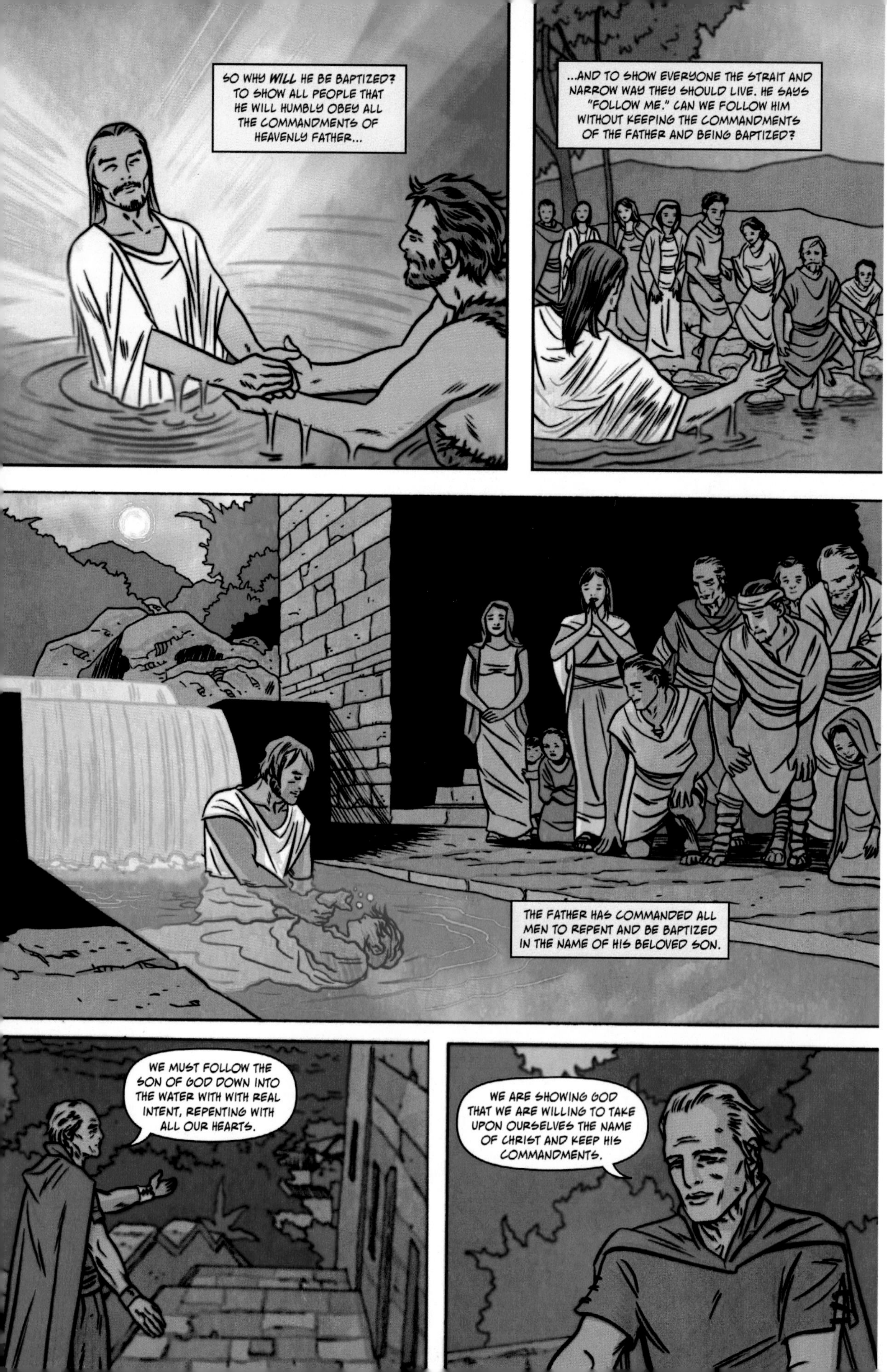

SO WHY WILL HE BE BAPTIZED? TO SHOW ALL PEOPLE THAT HE WILL HUMBLY OBEY ALL THE COMMANDMENTS OF HEAVENLY FATHER...
...AND TO SHOW EVERYONE THE STRAIT AND NARROW WAY THEY SHOULD LIVE. HE SAYS "FOLLOW ME." CAN WE FOLLOW HIM WITHOUT KEEPING THE COMMANDMENTS OF THE FATHER AND BEING BAPTIZED?
THE FATHER HAS COMMANDED ALL MEN TO REPENT AND BE BAPTIZED IN THE NAME OF HIS BELOVED SON.
WE MUST FOLLOW THE SON OF GOD DOWN INTO THE WATER WITH WITH REAL INTENT, REPENTING WITH ALL OUR HEARTS.
WE ARE SHOWING GOD THAT WE ARE WILLING TO TAKE UPON OURSELVES THE NAME OF CHRIST AND KEEP HIS COMMANDMENTS.

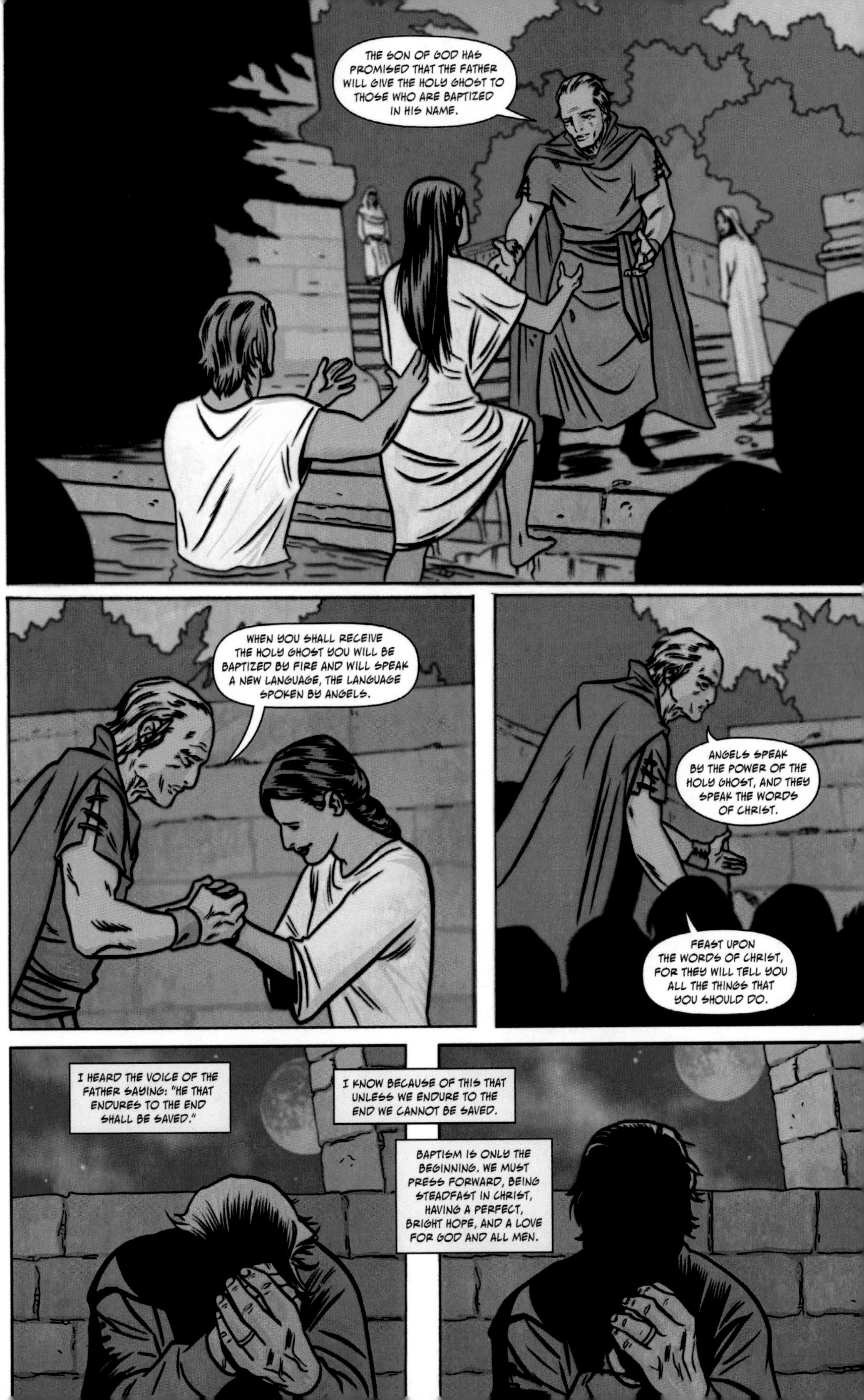
THE SON OF GOD HAS PROMISED THAT THE FATHER WILL GIVE THE HOLY GHOST TO THOSE WHO ARE BAPTIZED IN HIS NAME.
WHEN YOU SHALL RECEIVE THE HOLY GHOST YOU WILL BE BAPTIZED BY FIRE AND WILL SPEAK A NEW LANGUAGE, THE LANGUAGE SPOKEN BY ANGELS.
ANGELS SPEAK BY THE POWER OF THE HOLY GHOST, AND THEY SPEAK THE WORDS OF CHRIST.
FEAST UPON THE WORDS OF CHRIST, FOR THEY WILL TELL YOU ALL THE THINGS THAT YOU SHOULD DO.
I HEARD THE VOICE OF THE FATHER SAYING: "HE THAT ENDURES TO THE END SHALL BE SAVED."
I KNOW BECAUSE OF THIS THAT UNLESS WE ENDURE TO THE END WE CANNOT BE SAVED.
BAPTISM IS ONLY THE BEGINNING. WE MUST PRESS FORWARD, BEING STEADFAST IN CHRIST, HAVING A PERFECT, BRIGHT HOPE, AND A LOVE FOR GOD AND ALL MEN.

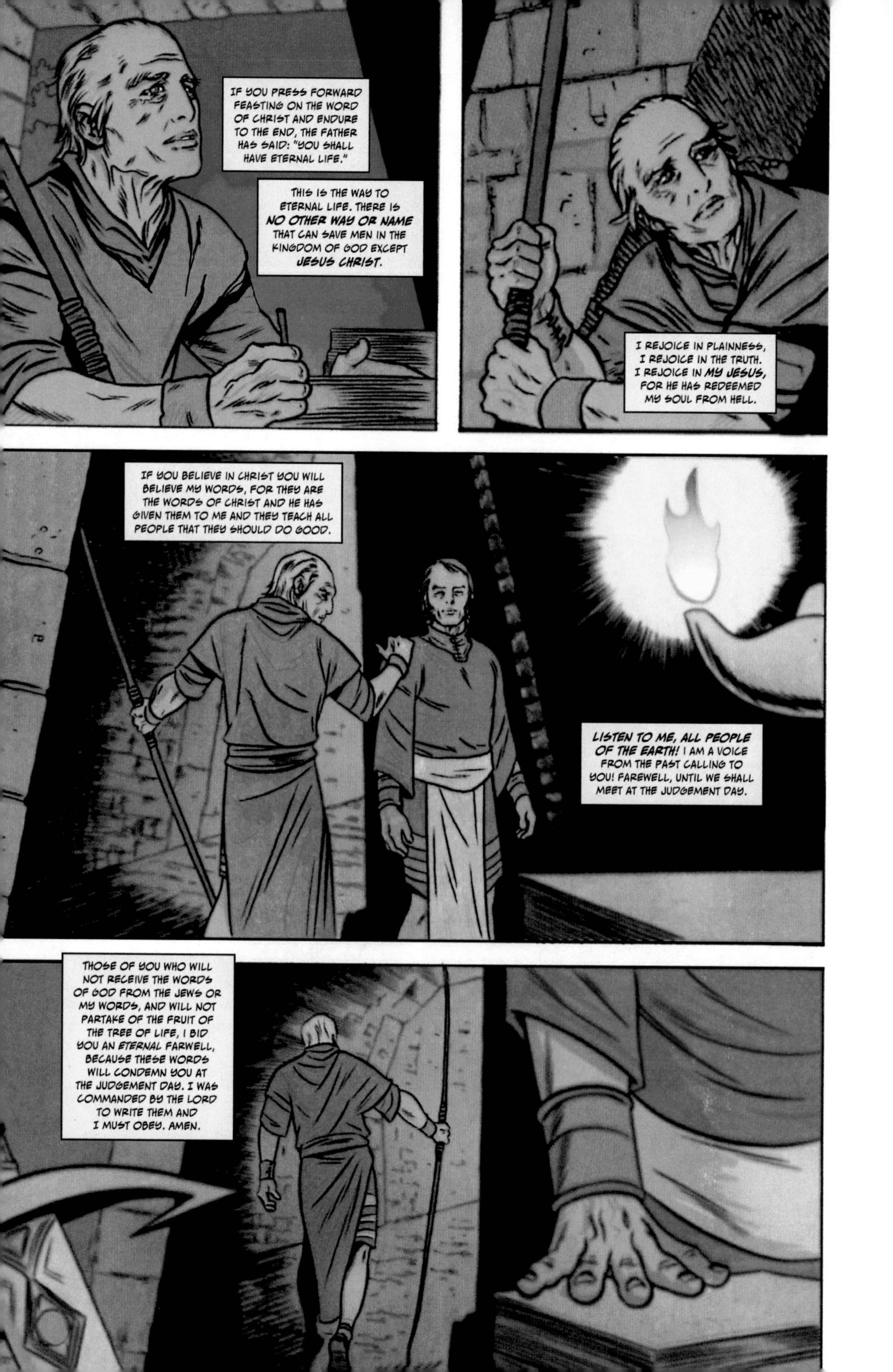
IF YOU PRESS FORWARD FEASTING ON THE WORD OF CHRIST AND ENDURE TO THE END, THE FATHER HAS SAID: "YOU SHALL HAVE ETERNAL LIFE."
THIS IS THE WAY TO ETERNAL LIFE. THERE IS NO OTHER WAY OR NAME THAT CAN SAVE MEN IN THE KINGDOM OF GOD EXCEPT JESUS CHRIST.
I REJOICE IN PLAINNESS, I REJOICE IN THE TRUTH. I REJOICE IN MY JESUS, FOR HE HAS REDEEMED MY SOUL FROM HELL.
IF YOU BELIEVE IN CHRIST YOU WILL BELIEVE MY WORDS, FOR THEY ARE THE WORDS OF CHRIST AND HE HAS GIVEN THEM TO ME AND THEY TEACH ALL PEOPLE THAT THEY SHOULD DO GOOD.
LISTEN TO ME, ALL PEOPLE OF THE EARTH! I AM A VOICE FROM THE PAST CALLING TO YOU! FAREWELL, UNTIL WE SHALL MEET AT THE JUDGEMENT DAY.
THOSE OF YOU WHO WILL NOT RECEIVE THE WORDS OF GOD FROM THE JEWS OR MY WORDS, AND WILL NOT PARTAKE OF THE FRUIT OF THE TREE OF LIFE, I BID YOU AN ETERNAL FARWELL, BECAUSE THESE WORDS WILL CONDEMN YOU AT THE JUDGEMENT DAY. I WAS COMMANDED BY THE LORD TO WRITE THEM AND I MUST OBEY. AMEN.

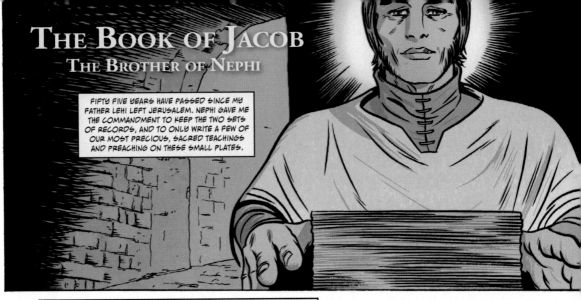

THE BOOK OF JACOB
THE BROTHER OF NEPHI

FIFTY FIVE YEARS HAVE PASSED SINCE MY FATHER LEHI LEFT JERUSALEM. NEPHI GAVE ME THE COMMANDMENT TO KEEP THE TWO SETS OF RECORDS, AND TO ONLY WRITE A FEW OF OUR MOST PRECIOUS, SACRED TEACHINGS AND PREACHING ON THESE SMALL PLATES.

WE HAD MANY REVELATIONS AND THE SPIRIT OF PROPHECY. WE LABORED TO PERSUADE OUR PEOPLE TO COME UNTO CHRIST AND PARTAKE OF HIS GOODNESS AND NOT REBEL AGAINST GOD AND PROVOKE HIM TO ANGER.

WHEN NEPHI WAS VERY OLD AND KNEW THAT HE WOULD SOON DIE, HE CHOSE A MAN TO BE THE NEXT KING.

NEPHI DIED THAT SAME YEAR.

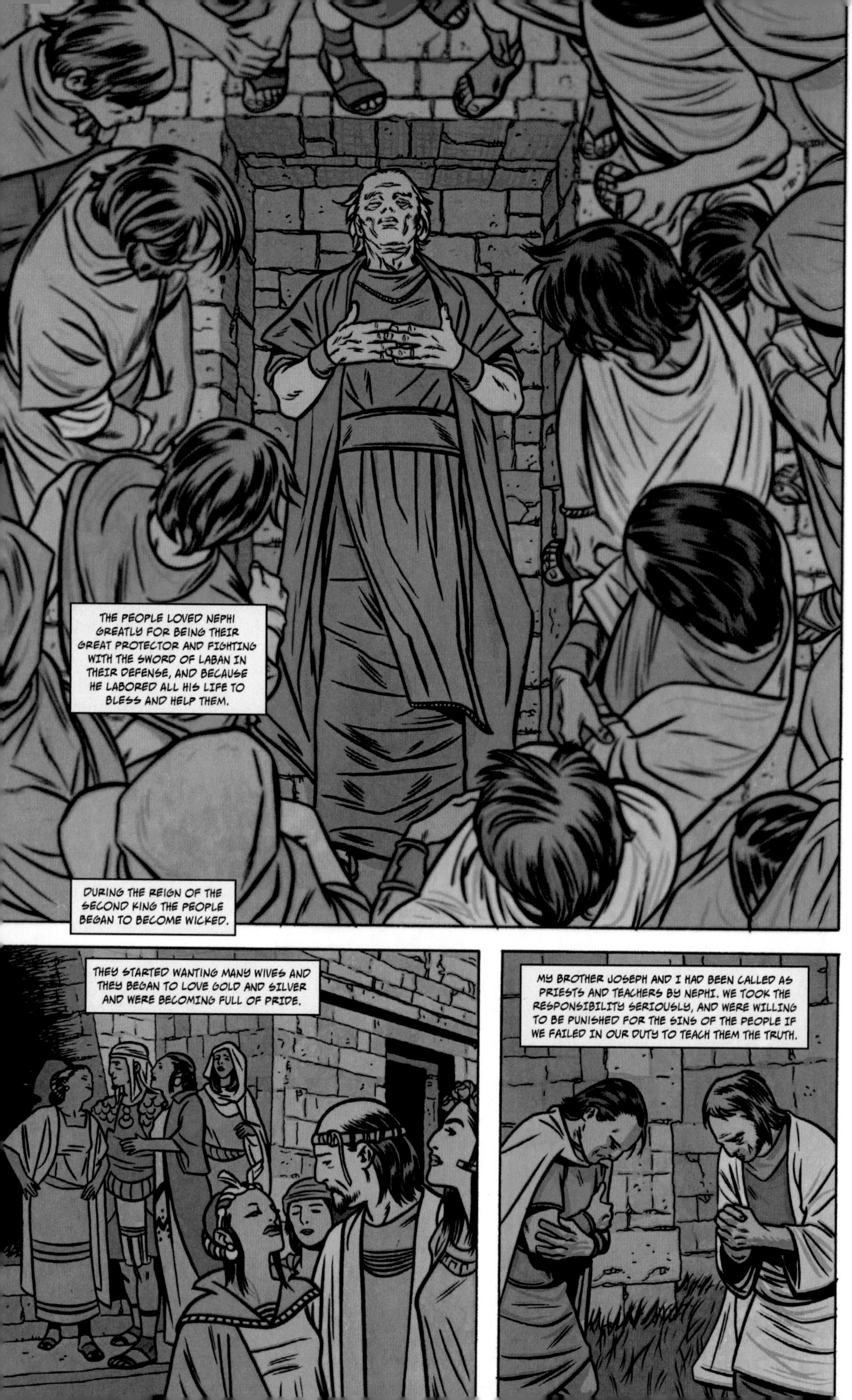
THE PEOPLE LOVED NEPHI GREATLY FOR BEING THEIR GREAT PROTECTOR AND FIGHTING WITH THE SWORD OF LABAN IN THEIR DEFENSE, AND BECAUSE HE LABORED ALL HIS LIFE TO BLESS AND HELP THEM.
DURING THE REIGN OF THE SECOND KING THE PEOPLE BEGAN TO BECOME WICKED.
THEY STARTED WANTING MANY WIVES AND THEY BEGAN TO LOVE GOLD AND SILVER AND WERE BECOMING FULL OF PRIDE.
MY BROTHER JOSEPH AND I HAD BEEN CALLED AS PRIESTS AND TEACHERS BY NEPHI. WE TOOK THE RESPONSIBILITY SERIOUSLY, AND WERE WILLING TO BE PUNISHED FOR THE SINS OF THE PEOPLE IF WE FAILED IN OUR DUTY TO TEACH THEM THE TRUTH.

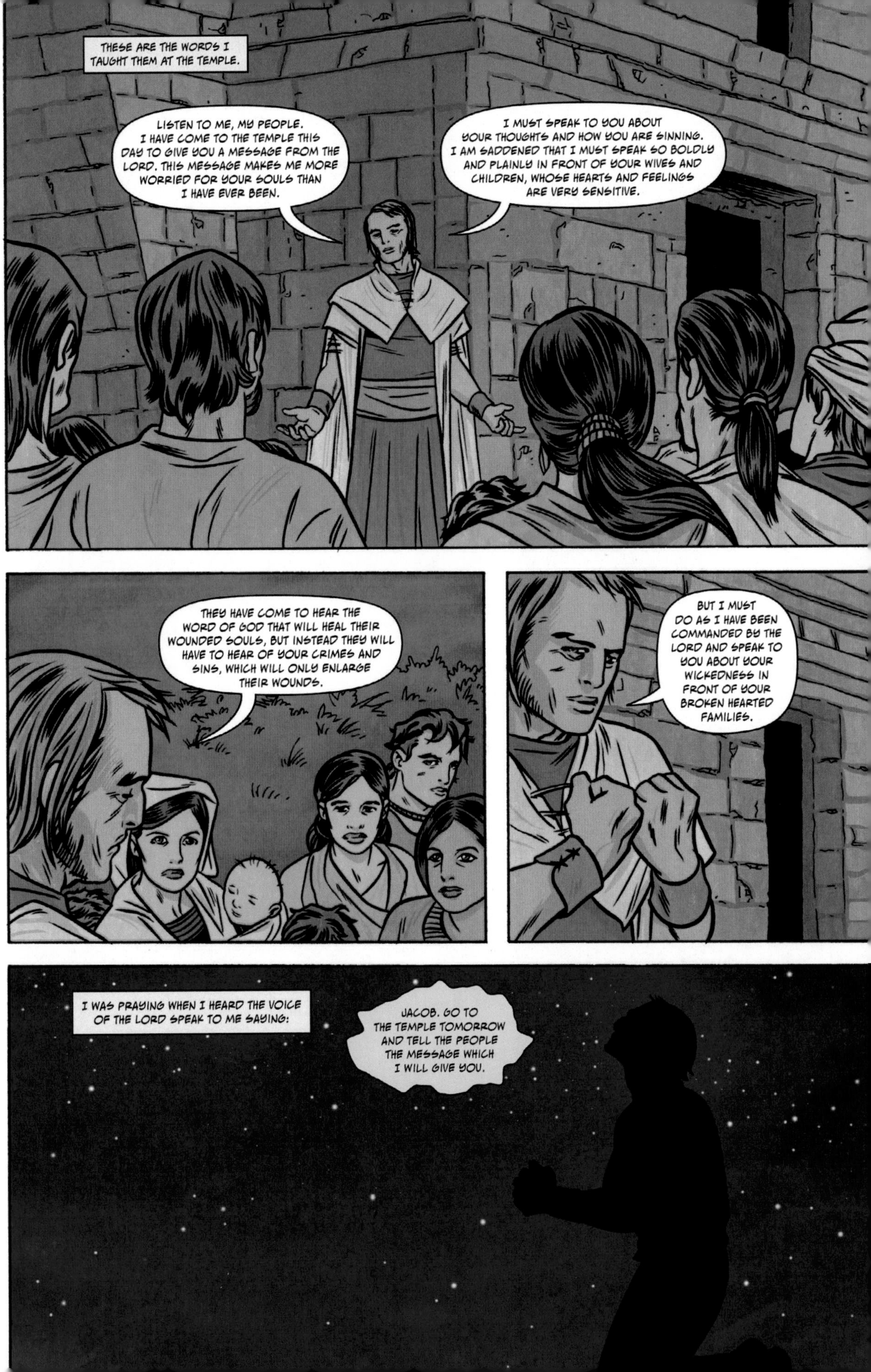
THESE ARE THE WORDS I TAUGHT THEM AT THE TEMPLE.
LISTEN TO ME, MY PEOPLE. I HAVE COME TO THE TEMPLE THIS DAY TO GIVE YOU A MESSAGE FROM THE LORD. THIS MESSAGE MAKES ME MORE WORRIED FOR YOUR SOULS THAN I HAVE EVER BEEN.
I MUST SPEAK TO YOU ABOUT YOUR THOUGHTS AND HOW YOU ARE SINNING. I AM SADDENED THAT I MUST SPEAK SO BOLDLY AND PLAINLY IN FRONT OF YOUR WIVES AND CHILDREN, WHOSE HEARTS AND FEELINGS ARE VERY SENSITIVE.
THEY HAVE COME TO HEAR THE WORD OF GOD THAT WILL HEAL THEIR WOUNDED SOULS, BUT INSTEAD THEY WILL HAVE TO HEAR OF YOUR CRIMES AND SINS, WHICH WILL ONLY ENLARGE THEIR WOUNDS.
BUT I MUST DO AS I HAVE BEEN COMMANDED BY THE LORD AND SPEAK TO YOU ABOUT YOUR WICKEDNESS IN FRONT OF YOUR BROKEN HEARTED FAMILIES.
I WAS PRAYING WHEN I HEARD THE VOICE OF THE LORD SPEAK TO ME SAYING:
JACOB. GO TO THE TEMPLE TOMORROW AND TELL THE PEOPLE THE MESSAGE WHICH I WILL GIVE YOU.

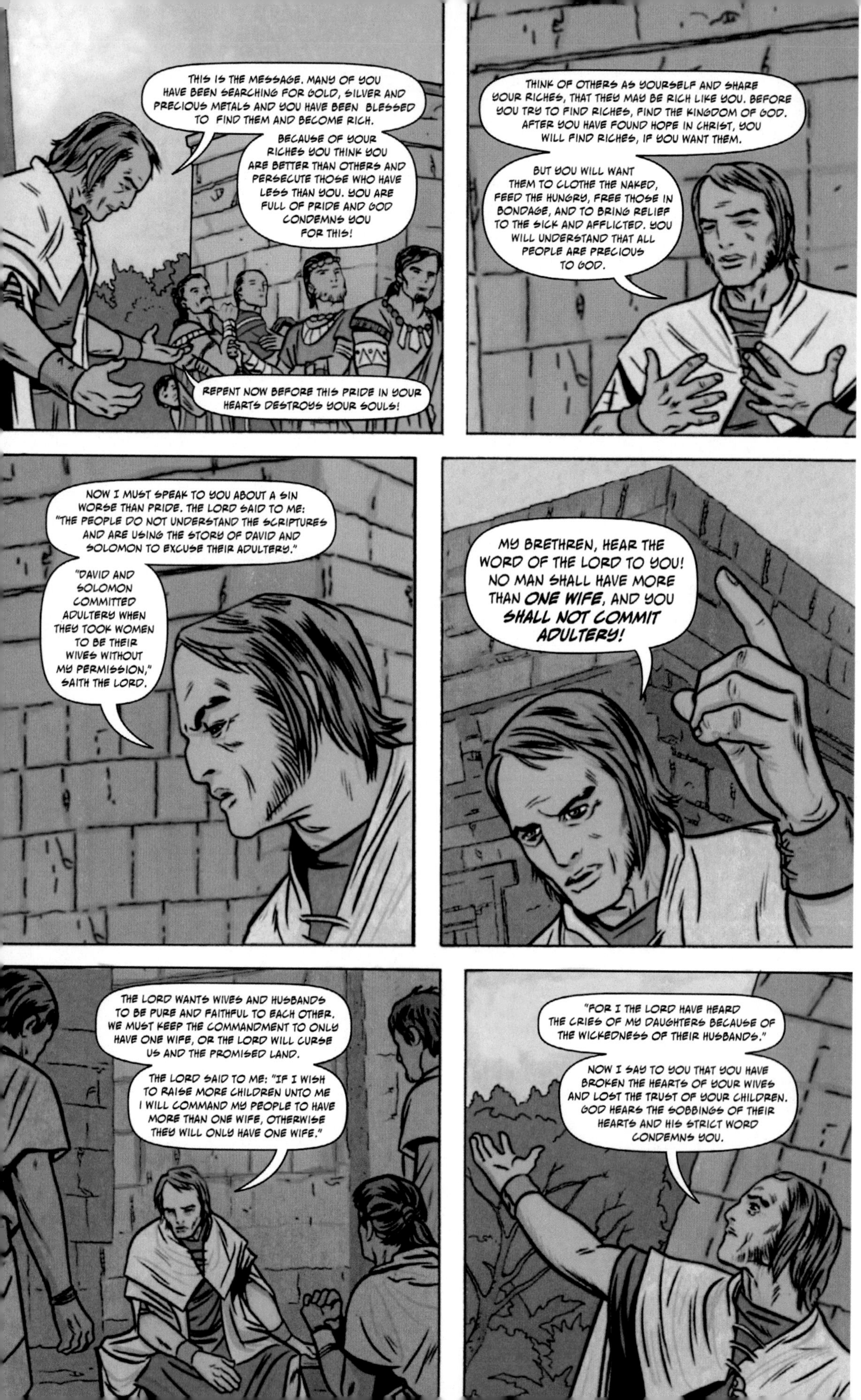
THIS IS THE MESSAGE. MANY OF YOU HAVE BEEN SEARCHING FOR GOLD, SILVER AND PRECIOUS METALS AND YOU HAVE BEEN BLESSED TO FIND THEM AND BECOME RICH.
BECAUSE OF YOUR RICHES YOU THINK YOU ARE BETTER THAN OTHERS AND PERSECUTE THOSE WHO HAVE LESS THAN YOU. YOU ARE FULL OF PRIDE AND GOD CONDEMNS YOU FOR THIS!
REPENT NOW BEFORE THIS PRIDE IN YOUR HEARTS DESTROYS YOUR SOULS!
THINK OF OTHERS AS YOURSELF AND SHARE YOUR RICHES, THAT THEY MAY BE RICH LIKE YOU. BEFORE YOU TRY TO FIND RICHES, FIND THE KINGDOM OF GOD. AFTER YOU HAVE FOUND HOPE IN CHRIST, YOU WILL FIND RICHES, IF YOU WANT THEM.
BUT YOU WILL WANT THEM TO CLOTHE THE NAKED, FEED THE HUNGRY, FREE THOSE IN BONDAGE, AND TO BRING RELIEF TO THE SICK AND AFFLICTED. YOU WILL UNDERSTAND THAT ALL PEOPLE ARE PRECIOUS TO GOD.
NOW I MUST SPEAK TO YOU ABOUT A SIN WORSE THAN PRIDE. THE LORD SAID TO ME: "THE PEOPLE DO NOT UNDERSTAND THE SCRIPTURES AND ARE USING THE STORY OF DAVID AND SOLOMON TO EXCUSE THEIR ADULTERY."
"DAVID AND SOLOMON COMMITTED ADULTERY WHEN THEY TOOK WOMEN TO BE THEIR WIVES WITHOUT MY PERMISSION," SAITH THE LORD.
MY BRETHREN, HEAR THE WORD OF THE LORD TO YOU! NO MAN SHALL HAVE MORE THAN ***ONE WIFE***, AND YOU ***SHALL NOT COMMIT ADULTERY!***
THE LORD WANTS WIVES AND HUSBANDS TO BE PURE AND FAITHFUL TO EACH OTHER. WE MUST KEEP THE COMMANDMENT TO ONLY HAVE ONE WIFE, OR THE LORD WILL CURSE US AND THE PROMISED LAND.
THE LORD SAID TO ME: "IF I WISH TO RAISE MORE CHILDREN UNTO ME I WILL COMMAND MY PEOPLE TO HAVE MORE THAN ONE WIFE, OTHERWISE THEY WILL ONLY HAVE ONE WIFE."
"FOR I THE LORD HAVE HEARD THE CRIES OF MY DAUGHTERS BECAUSE OF THE WICKEDNESS OF THEIR HUSBANDS."
NOW I SAY TO YOU THAT YOU HAVE BROKEN THE HEARTS OF YOUR WIVES AND LOST THE TRUST OF YOUR CHILDREN. GOD HEARS THE SOBBINGS OF THEIR HEARTS AND HIS STRICT WORD CONDEMNS YOU.

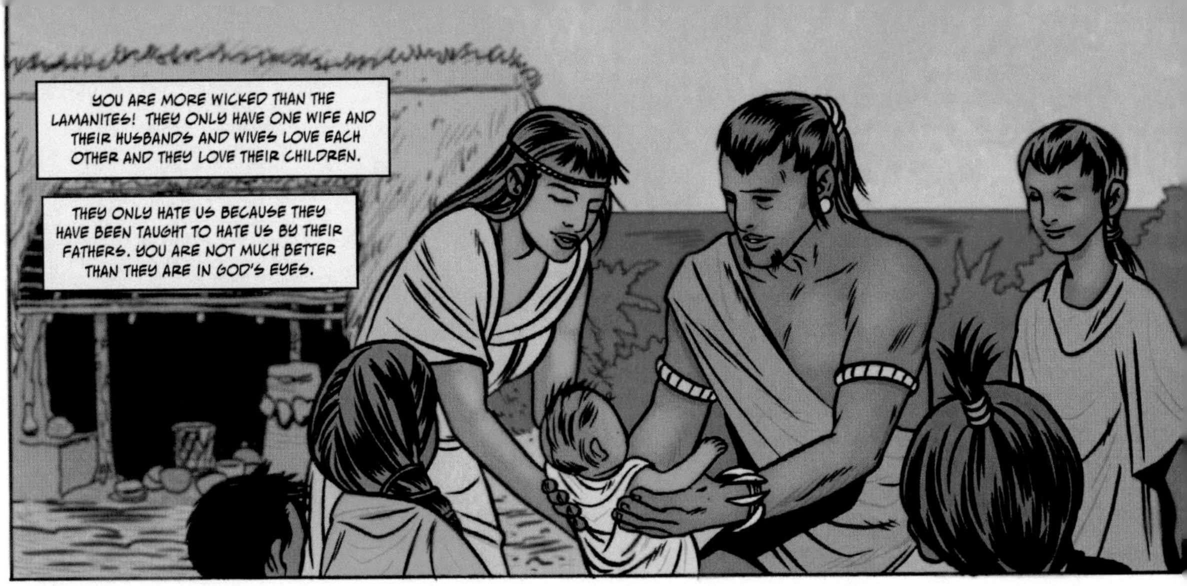
YOU ARE MORE WICKED THAN THE LAMANITES! THEY ONLY HAVE ONE WIFE AND THEIR HUSBANDS AND WIVES LOVE EACH OTHER AND THEY LOVE THEIR CHILDREN.
THEY ONLY HATE US BECAUSE THEY HAVE BEEN TAUGHT TO HATE US BY THEIR FATHERS. YOU ARE NOT MUCH BETTER THAN THEY ARE IN GOD'S EYES.

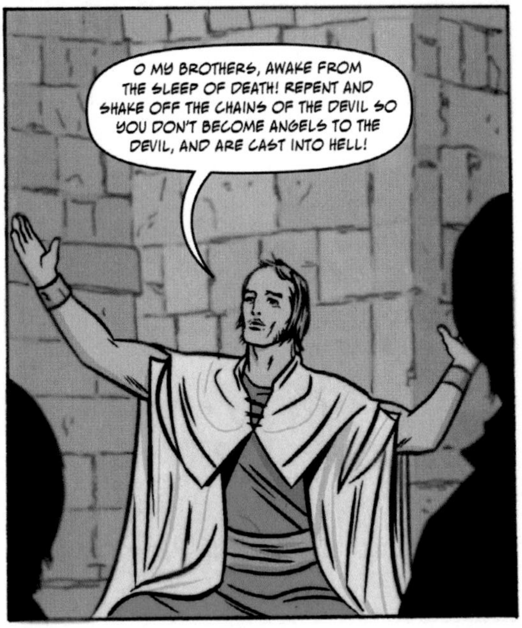
O MY BROTHERS, AWAKE FROM THE SLEEP OF DEATH! REPENT AND SHAKE OFF THE CHAINS OF THE DEVIL SO YOU DON'T BECOME ANGELS TO THE DEVIL, AND ARE CAST INTO HELL!

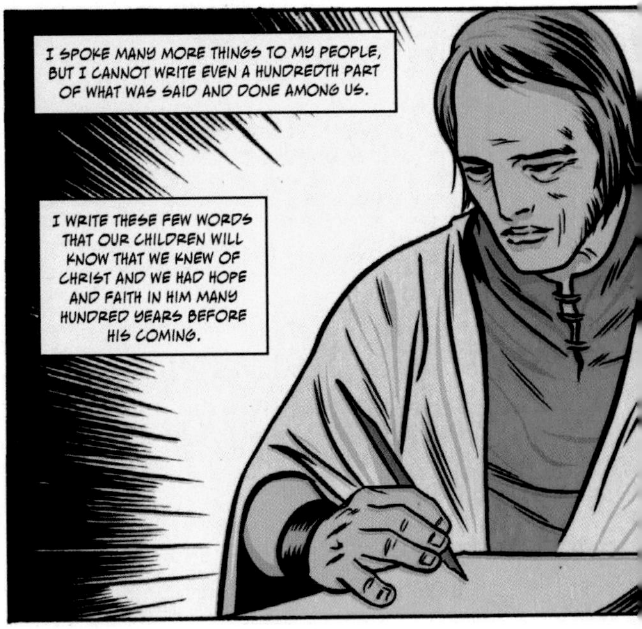
I SPOKE MANY MORE THINGS TO MY PEOPLE, BUT I CANNOT WRITE EVEN A HUNDREDTH PART OF WHAT WAS SAID AND DONE AMONG US.
I WRITE THESE FEW WORDS THAT OUR CHILDREN WILL KNOW THAT WE KNEW OF CHRIST AND WE HAD HOPE AND FAITH IN HIM MANY HUNDRED YEARS BEFORE HIS COMING.

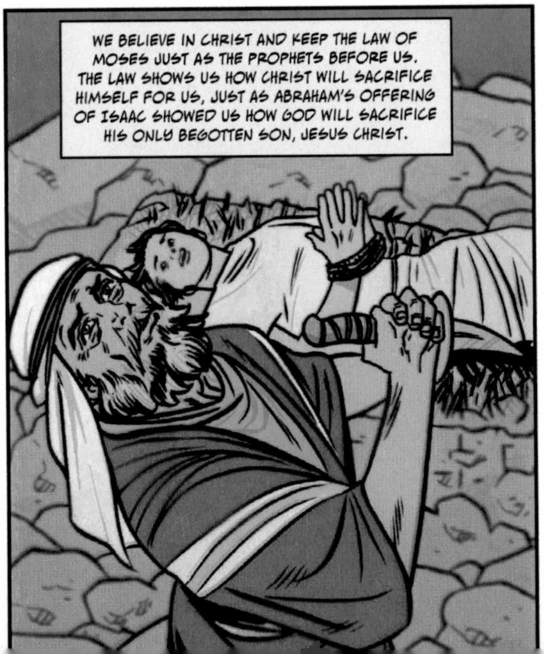
WE BELIEVE IN CHRIST AND KEEP THE LAW OF MOSES JUST AS THE PROPHETS BEFORE US. THE LAW SHOWS US HOW CHRIST WILL SACRIFICE HIMSELF FOR US, JUST AS ABRAHAM'S OFFERING OF ISAAC SHOWED US HOW GOD WILL SACRIFICE HIS ONLY BEGOTTEN SON, JESUS CHRIST.

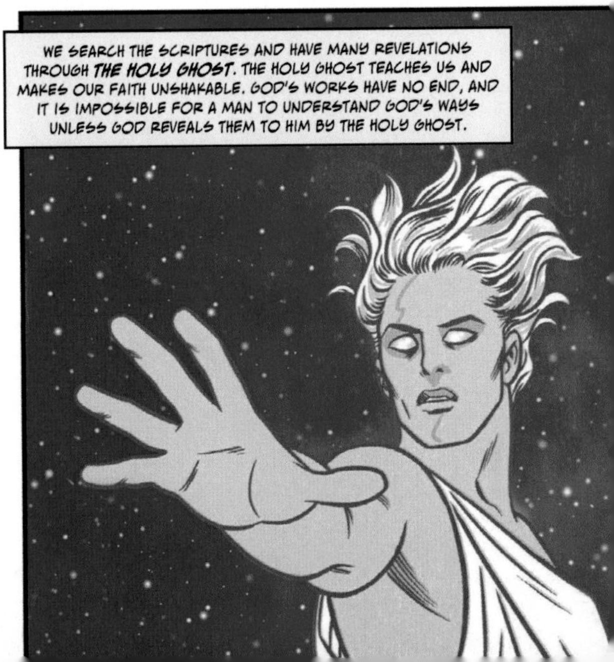
WE SEARCH THE SCRIPTURES AND HAVE MANY REVELATIONS THROUGH *THE HOLY GHOST*. THE HOLY GHOST TEACHES US AND MAKES OUR FAITH UNSHAKABLE. GOD'S WORKS HAVE NO END, AND IT IS IMPOSSIBLE FOR A MAN TO UNDERSTAND GOD'S WAYS UNLESS GOD REVEALS THEM TO HIM BY THE HOLY GHOST.

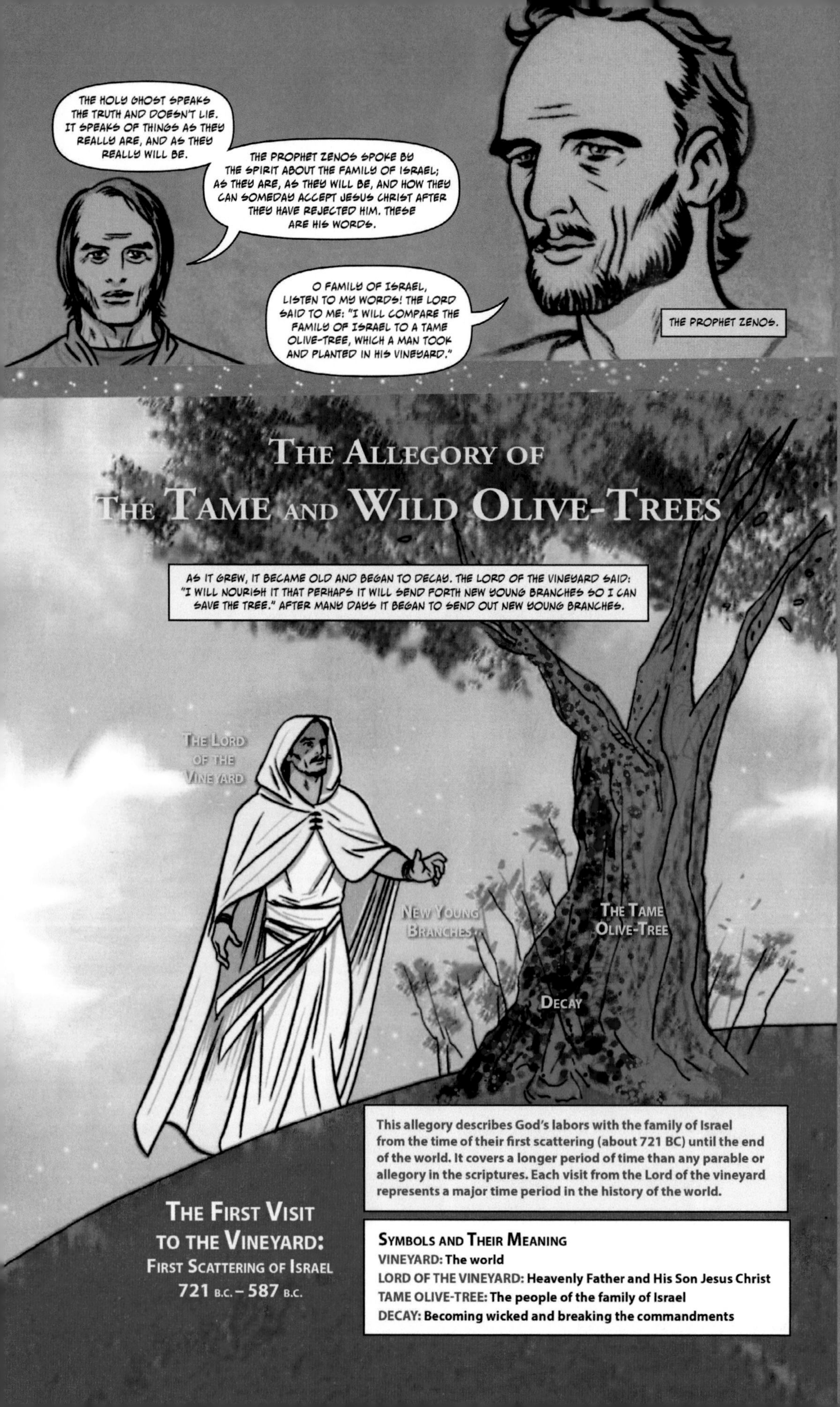
THE HOLY GHOST SPEAKS THE TRUTH AND DOESN'T LIE. IT SPEAKS OF THINGS AS THEY REALLY ARE, AND AS THEY REALLY WILL BE.
THE PROPHET ZENOS SPOKE BY THE SPIRIT ABOUT THE FAMILY OF ISRAEL; AS THEY ARE, AS THEY WILL BE, AND HOW THEY CAN SOMEDAY ACCEPT JESUS CHRIST AFTER THEY HAVE REJECTED HIM. THESE ARE HIS WORDS.
O FAMILY OF ISRAEL, LISTEN TO MY WORDS! THE LORD SAID TO ME: "I WILL COMPARE THE FAMILY OF ISRAEL TO A TAME OLIVE-TREE, WHICH A MAN TOOK AND PLANTED IN HIS VINEYARD."
THE PROPHET ZENOS.
THE ALLEGORY OF THE TAME AND WILD OLIVE-TREES
AS IT GREW, IT BECAME OLD AND BEGAN TO DECAY. THE LORD OF THE VINEYARD SAID: "I WILL NOURISH IT THAT PERHAPS IT WILL SEND FORTH NEW YOUNG BRANCHES SO I CAN SAVE THE TREE." AFTER MANY DAYS IT BEGAN TO SEND OUT NEW YOUNG BRANCHES.
THE LORD OF THE VINEYARD
NEW YOUNG BRANCHES
THE TAME OLIVE-TREE
DECAY
This allegory describes God's labors with the family of Israel from the time of their first scattering (about 721 BC) until the end of the world. It covers a longer period of time than any parable or allegory in the scriptures. Each visit from the Lord of the vineyard represents a major time period in the history of the world.
THE FIRST VISIT TO THE VINEYARD:
FIRST SCATTERING OF ISRAEL
721 B.C. – 587 B.C.
SYMBOLS AND THEIR MEANING
VINEYARD: The world
LORD OF THE VINEYARD: Heavenly Father and His Son Jesus Christ
TAME OLIVE-TREE: The people of the family of Israel
DECAY: Becoming wicked and breaking the commandments

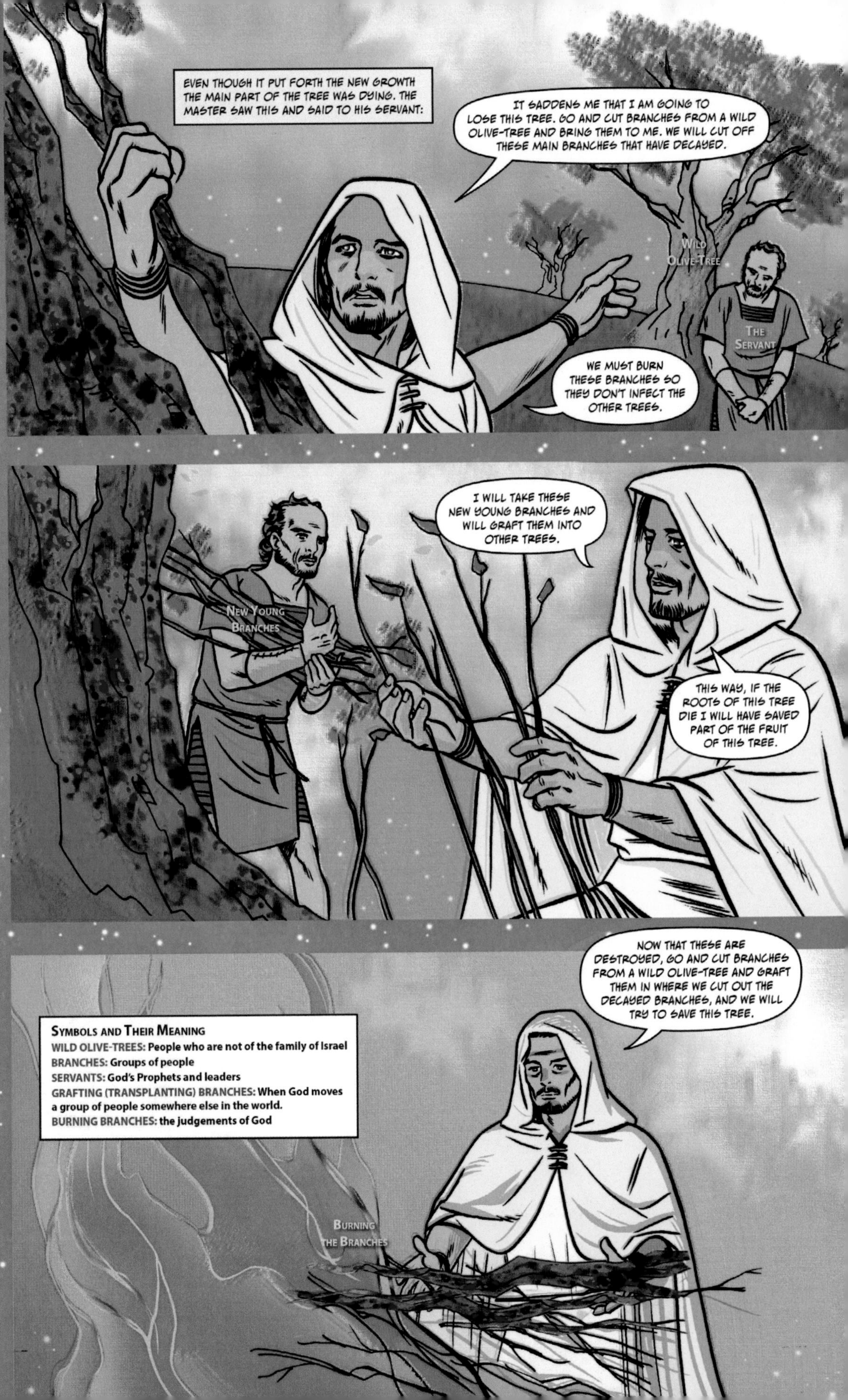

EVEN THOUGH IT PUT FORTH THE NEW GROWTH THE MAIN PART OF THE TREE WAS DYING. THE MASTER SAW THIS AND SAID TO HIS SERVANT:
IT SADDENS ME THAT I AM GOING TO LOSE THIS TREE. GO AND CUT BRANCHES FROM A WILD OLIVE-TREE AND BRING THEM TO ME. WE WILL CUT OFF THESE MAIN BRANCHES THAT HAVE DECAYED.
Wild Olive-Tree
The Servant
WE MUST BURN THESE BRANCHES SO THEY DON'T INFECT THE OTHER TREES.
New Young Branches
I WILL TAKE THESE NEW YOUNG BRANCHES AND WILL GRAFT THEM INTO OTHER TREES.
THIS WAY, IF THE ROOTS OF THIS TREE DIE I WILL HAVE SAVED PART OF THE FRUIT OF THIS TREE.
NOW THAT THESE ARE DESTROYED, GO AND CUT BRANCHES FROM A WILD OLIVE-TREE AND GRAFT THEM IN WHERE WE CUT OUT THE DECAYED BRANCHES, AND WE WILL TRY TO SAVE THIS TREE.
Symbols and Their Meaning
WILD OLIVE-TREES: People who are not of the family of Israel
BRANCHES: Groups of people
SERVANTS: God's Prophets and leaders
GRAFTING (TRANSPLANTING) BRANCHES: When God moves a group of people somewhere else in the world.
BURNING BRANCHES: the judgements of God
Burning the Branches

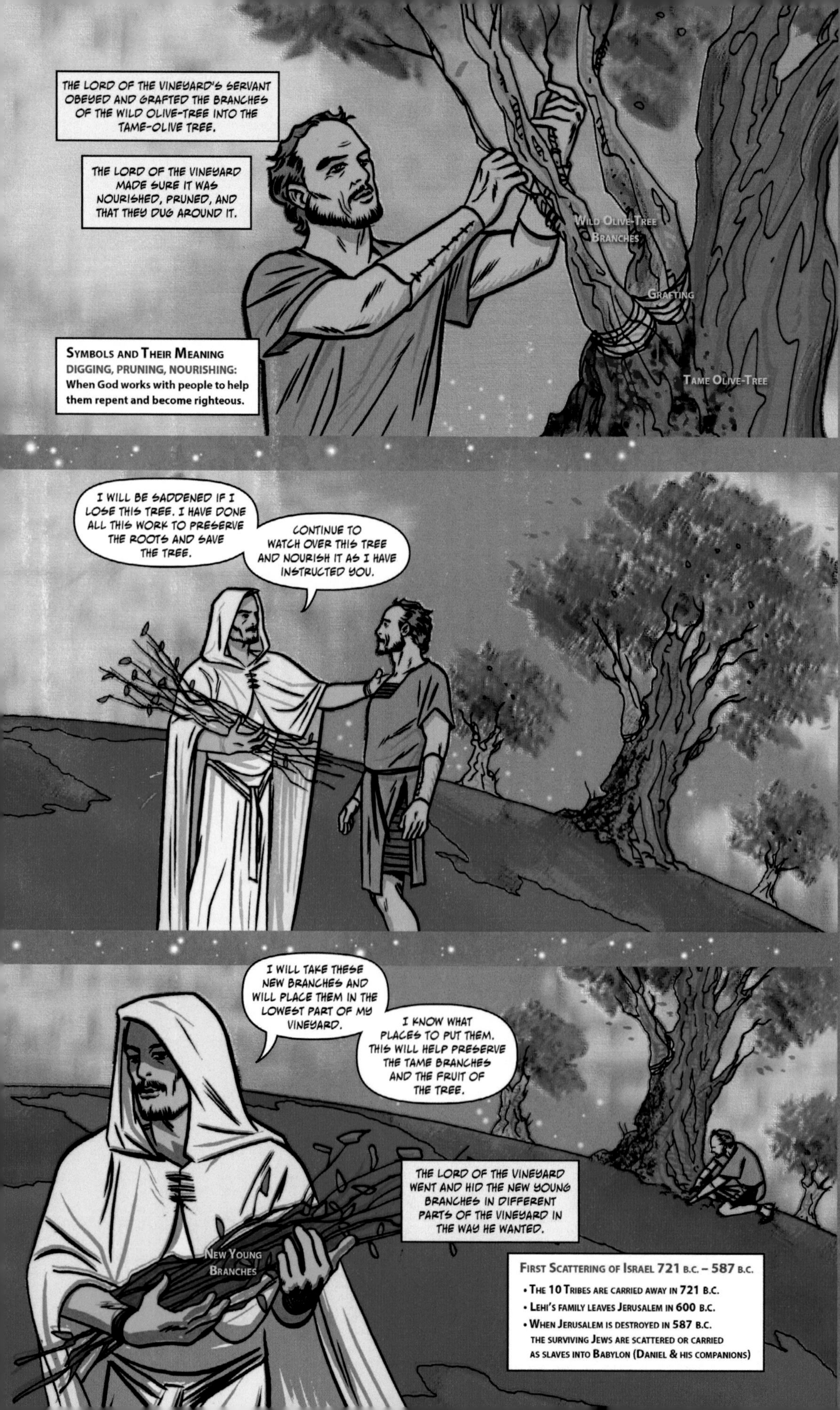

THE LORD OF THE VINEYARD'S SERVANT OBEYED AND GRAFTED THE BRANCHES OF THE WILD OLIVE-TREE INTO THE TAME-OLIVE TREE.
THE LORD OF THE VINEYARD MADE SURE IT WAS NOURISHED, PRUNED, AND THAT THEY DUG AROUND IT.
WILD OLIVE-TREE BRANCHES
GRAFTING
TAME OLIVE-TREE
SYMBOLS AND THEIR MEANING
DIGGING, PRUNING, NOURISHING:
When God works with people to help them repent and become righteous.
I WILL BE SADDENED IF I LOSE THIS TREE. I HAVE DONE ALL THIS WORK TO PRESERVE THE ROOTS AND SAVE THE TREE.
CONTINUE TO WATCH OVER THIS TREE AND NOURISH IT AS I HAVE INSTRUCTED YOU.
I WILL TAKE THESE NEW BRANCHES AND WILL PLACE THEM IN THE LOWEST PART OF MY VINEYARD.
I KNOW WHAT PLACES TO PUT THEM. THIS WILL HELP PRESERVE THE TAME BRANCHES AND THE FRUIT OF THE TREE.
THE LORD OF THE VINEYARD WENT AND HID THE NEW YOUNG BRANCHES IN DIFFERENT PARTS OF THE VINEYARD IN THE WAY HE WANTED.
NEW YOUNG BRANCHES
FIRST SCATTERING OF ISRAEL 721 B.C. – 587 B.C.
• THE 10 TRIBES ARE CARRIED AWAY IN 721 B.C.
• LEHI'S FAMILY LEAVES JERUSALEM IN 600 B.C.
• WHEN JERUSALEM IS DESTROYED IN 587 B.C. THE SURVIVING JEWS ARE SCATTERED OR CARRIED AS SLAVES INTO BABYLON (DANIEL & HIS COMPANIONS)

The Second Visit to the Vineyard:
The time of Christ's Life on Earth (about 30 A.D.)

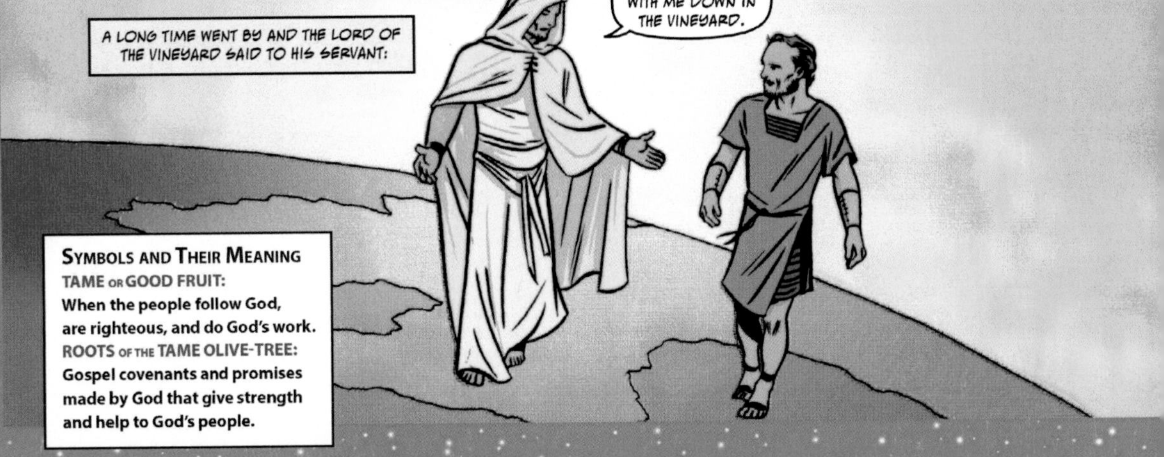
A LONG TIME WENT BY AND THE LORD OF THE VINEYARD SAID TO HIS SERVANT:
COME AND WORK WITH ME DOWN IN THE VINEYARD.
SYMBOLS AND THEIR MEANING
TAME OR GOOD FRUIT:
When the people follow God, are righteous, and do God's work.
ROOTS OF THE TAME OLIVE-TREE:
Gospel covenants and promises made by God that give strength and help to God's people.

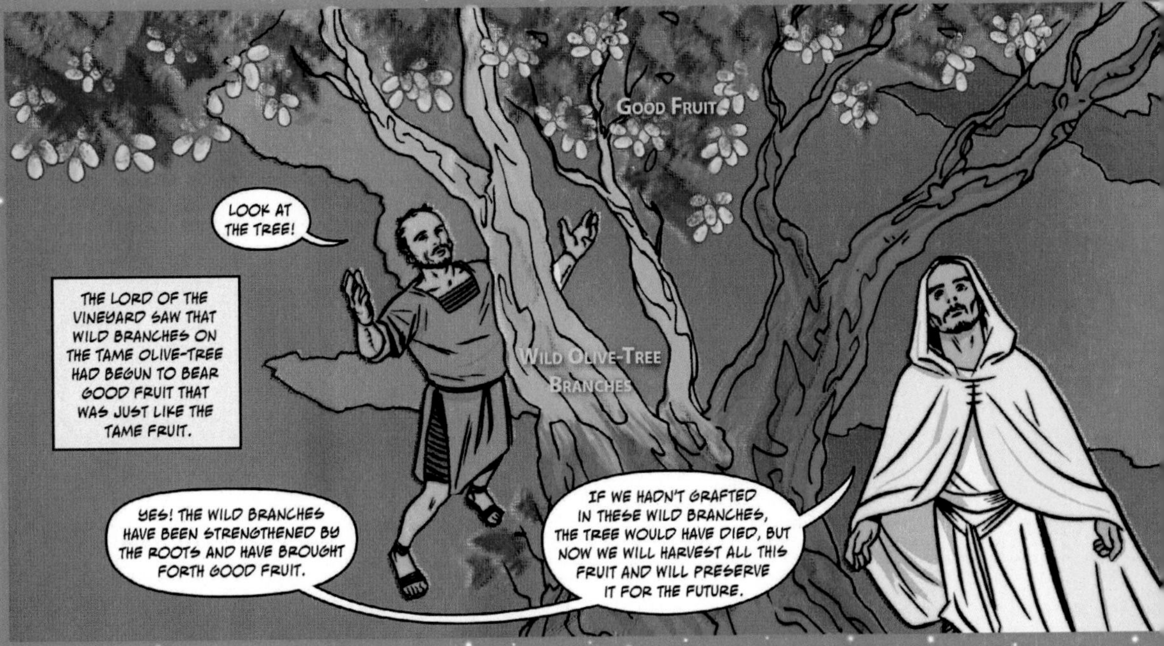
GOOD FRUIT
LOOK AT THE TREE!
THE LORD OF THE VINEYARD SAW THAT WILD BRANCHES ON THE TAME OLIVE-TREE HAD BEGUN TO BEAR GOOD FRUIT THAT WAS JUST LIKE THE TAME FRUIT.
WILD OLIVE-TREE BRANCHES
YES! THE WILD BRANCHES HAVE BEEN STRENGTHENED BY THE ROOTS AND HAVE BROUGHT FORTH GOOD FRUIT.
IF WE HADN'T GRAFTED IN THESE WILD BRANCHES, THE TREE WOULD HAVE DIED, BUT NOW WE WILL HARVEST ALL THIS FRUIT AND WILL PRESERVE IT FOR THE FUTURE.

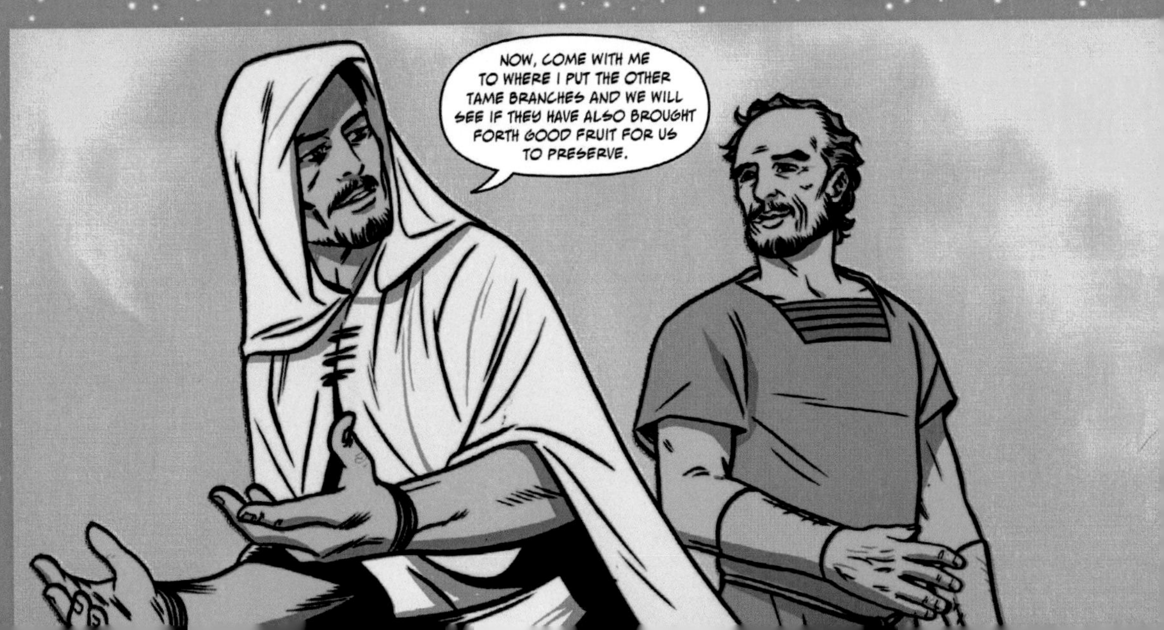
NOW, COME WITH ME TO WHERE I PUT THE OTHER TAME BRANCHES AND WE WILL SEE IF THEY HAVE ALSO BROUGHT FORTH GOOD FRUIT FOR US TO PRESERVE.

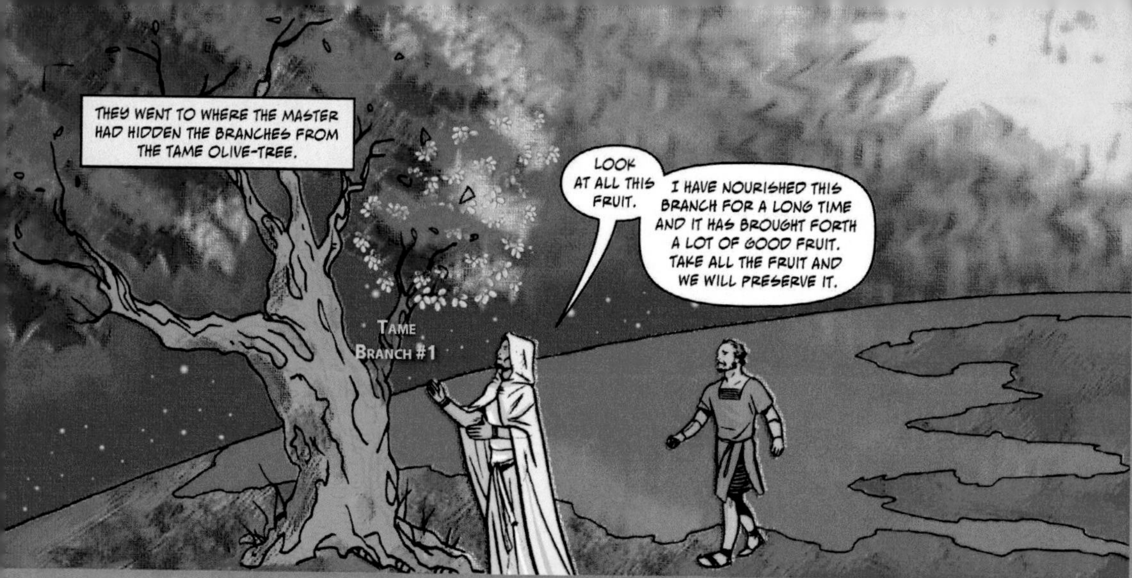
THEY WENT TO WHERE THE MASTER HAD HIDDEN THE BRANCHES FROM THE TAME OLIVE-TREE.
LOOK AT ALL THIS FRUIT.
I HAVE NOURISHED THIS BRANCH FOR A LONG TIME AND IT HAS BROUGHT FORTH A LOT OF GOOD FRUIT. TAKE ALL THE FRUIT AND WE WILL PRESERVE IT.
TAME BRANCH #1

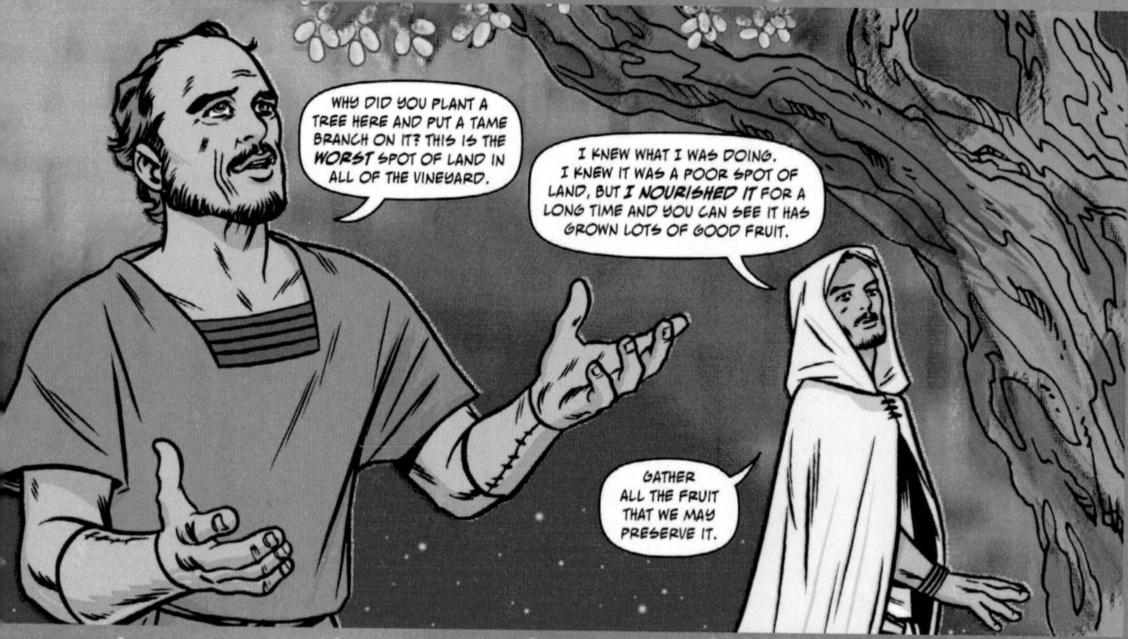
WHY DID YOU PLANT A TREE HERE AND PUT A TAME BRANCH ON IT? THIS IS THE *WORST* SPOT OF LAND IN ALL OF THE VINEYARD.
I KNEW WHAT I WAS DOING. I KNEW IT WAS A POOR SPOT OF LAND, BUT *I NOURISHED IT* FOR A LONG TIME AND YOU CAN SEE IT HAS GROWN LOTS OF GOOD FRUIT.
GATHER ALL THE FRUIT THAT WE MAY PRESERVE IT.

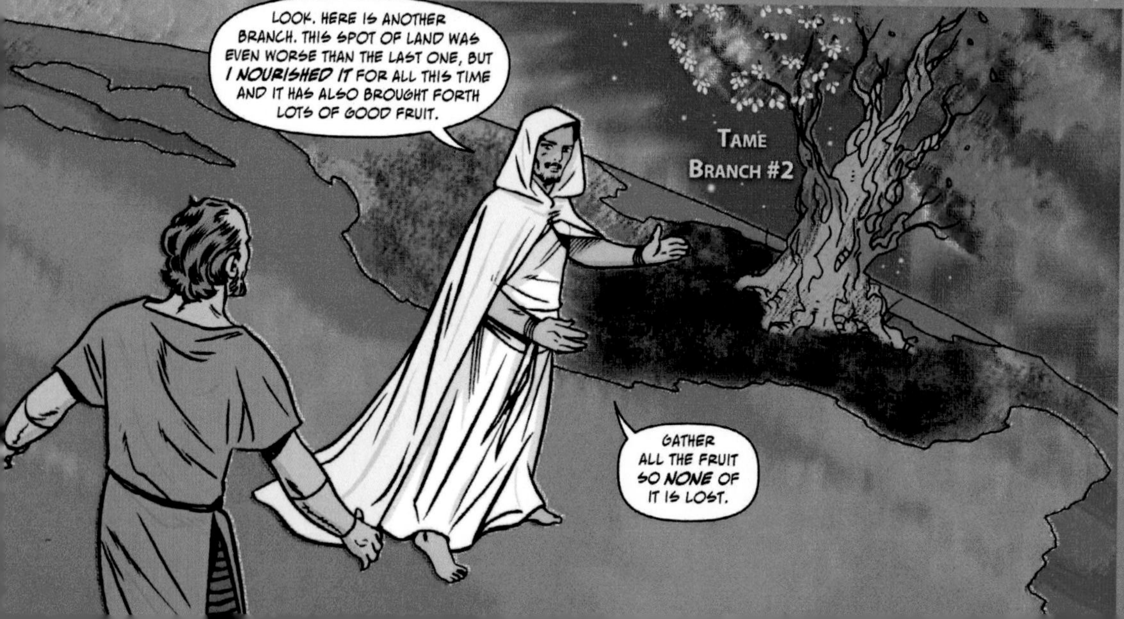
LOOK. HERE IS ANOTHER BRANCH. THIS SPOT OF LAND WAS EVEN WORSE THAN THE LAST ONE, BUT *I NOURISHED IT* FOR ALL THIS TIME AND IT HAS ALSO BROUGHT FORTH LOTS OF GOOD FRUIT.
TAME BRANCH #2
GATHER ALL THE FRUIT SO *NONE* OF IT IS LOST.

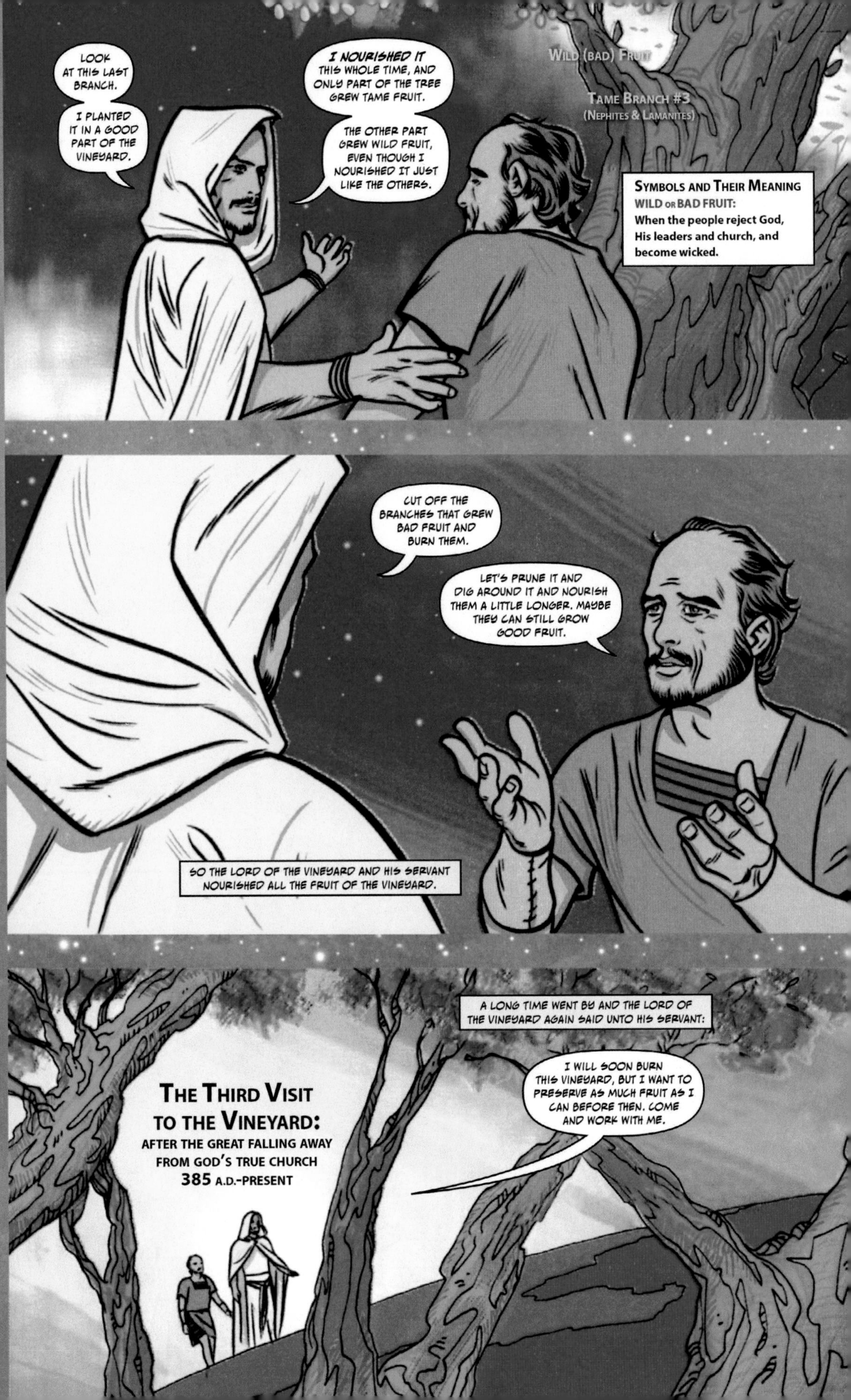

LOOK AT THIS LAST BRANCH.
I PLANTED IT IN A GOOD PART OF THE VINEYARD.
I NOURISHED IT THIS WHOLE TIME, AND ONLY PART OF THE TREE GREW TAME FRUIT.
THE OTHER PART GREW WILD FRUIT, EVEN THOUGH I NOURISHED IT JUST LIKE THE OTHERS.
Wild (bad) Fruit
Tame Branch #3
(Nephites & Lamanites)
Symbols and Their Meaning
WILD or BAD FRUIT:
When the people reject God, His leaders and church, and become wicked.
CUT OFF THE BRANCHES THAT GREW BAD FRUIT AND BURN THEM.
LET'S PRUNE IT AND DIG AROUND IT AND NOURISH THEM A LITTLE LONGER. MAYBE THEY CAN STILL GROW GOOD FRUIT.
SO THE LORD OF THE VINEYARD AND HIS SERVANT NOURISHED ALL THE FRUIT OF THE VINEYARD.
A LONG TIME WENT BY AND THE LORD OF THE VINEYARD AGAIN SAID UNTO HIS SERVANT:
The Third Visit to the Vineyard:
AFTER THE GREAT FALLING AWAY FROM GOD'S TRUE CHURCH
385 A.D.-PRESENT
I WILL SOON BURN THIS VINEYARD, BUT I WANT TO PRESERVE AS MUCH FRUIT AS I CAN BEFORE THEN. COME AND WORK WITH ME.

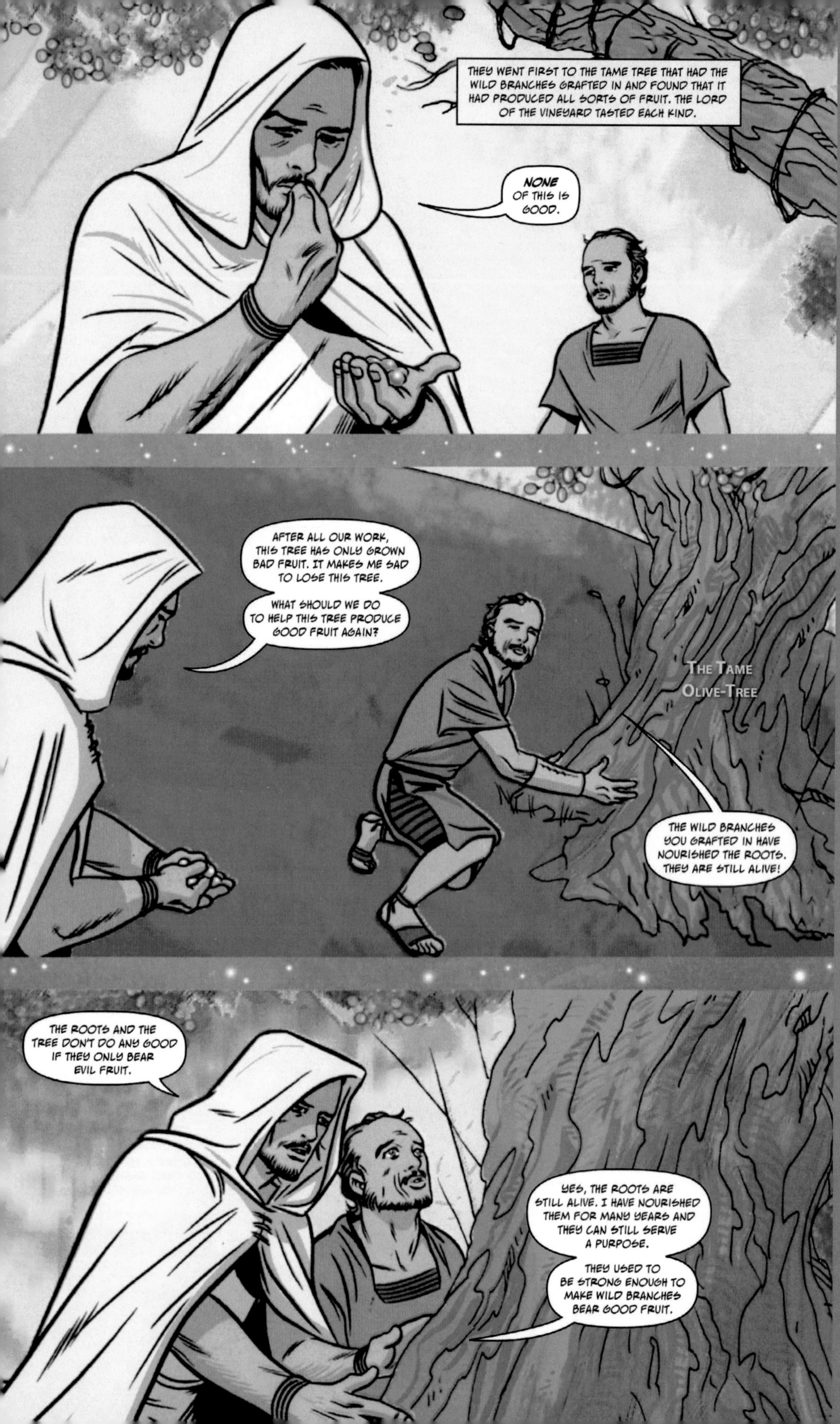
THEY WENT FIRST TO THE TAME TREE THAT HAD THE WILD BRANCHES GRAFTED IN AND FOUND THAT IT HAD PRODUCED ALL SORTS OF FRUIT. THE LORD OF THE VINEYARD TASTED EACH KIND.
NONE OF THIS IS GOOD.
AFTER ALL OUR WORK, THIS TREE HAS ONLY GROWN BAD FRUIT. IT MAKES ME SAD TO LOSE THIS TREE.
WHAT SHOULD WE DO TO HELP THIS TREE PRODUCE GOOD FRUIT AGAIN?
THE TAME OLIVE-TREE
THE WILD BRANCHES YOU GRAFTED IN HAVE NOURISHED THE ROOTS. THEY ARE STILL ALIVE!
THE ROOTS AND THE TREE DON'T DO ANY GOOD IF THEY ONLY BEAR EVIL FRUIT.
YES, THE ROOTS ARE STILL ALIVE. I HAVE NOURISHED THEM FOR MANY YEARS AND THEY CAN STILL SERVE A PURPOSE.
THEY USED TO BE STRONG ENOUGH TO MAKE WILD BRANCHES BEAR GOOD FRUIT.

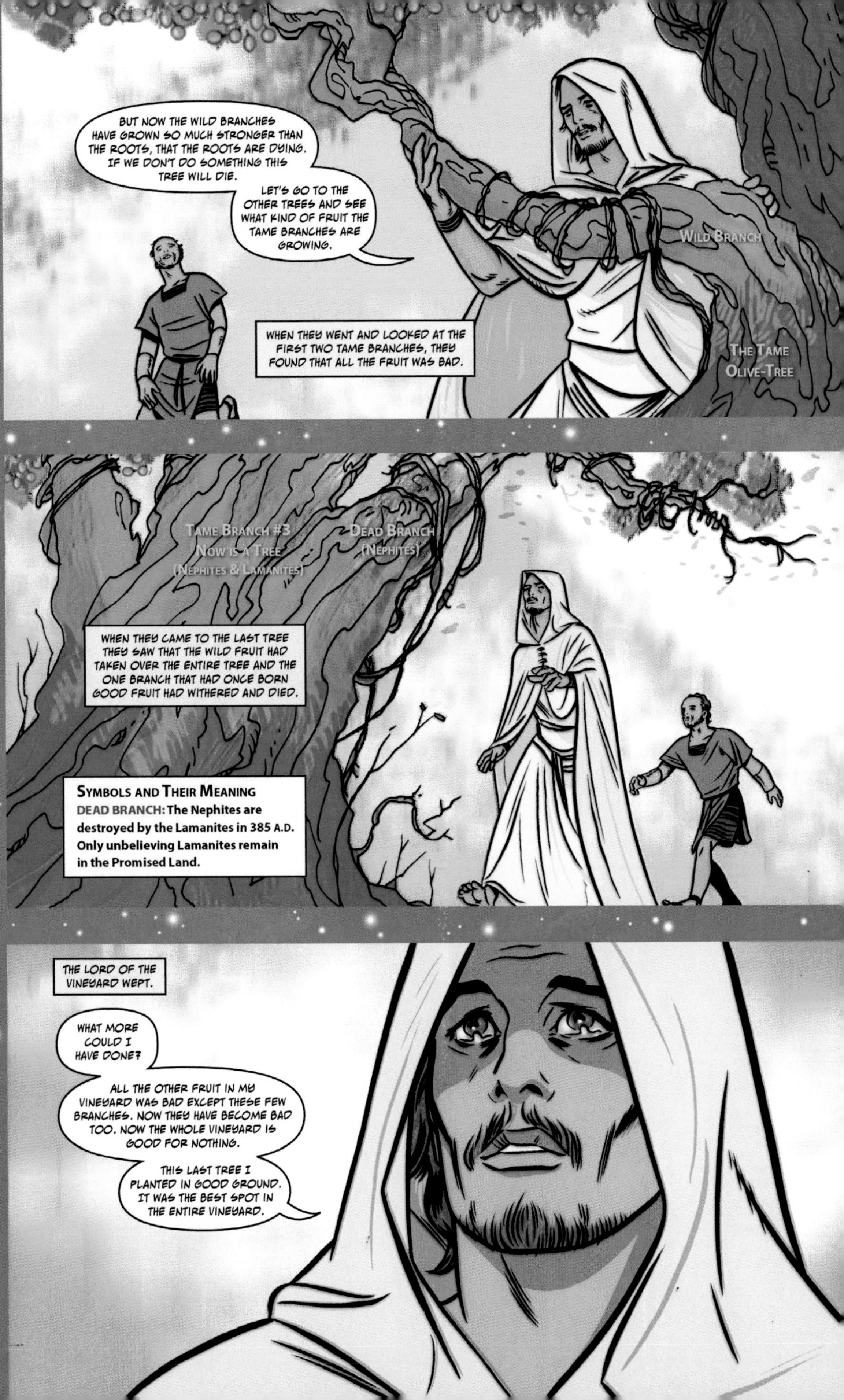

BUT NOW THE WILD BRANCHES HAVE GROWN SO MUCH STRONGER THAN THE ROOTS, THAT THE ROOTS ARE DYING. IF WE DON'T DO SOMETHING THIS TREE WILL DIE.
LET'S GO TO THE OTHER TREES AND SEE WHAT KIND OF FRUIT THE TAME BRANCHES ARE GROWING.
WILD BRANCH
WHEN THEY WENT AND LOOKED AT THE FIRST TWO TAME BRANCHES, THEY FOUND THAT ALL THE FRUIT WAS BAD.
THE TAME OLIVE-TREE
TAME BRANCH #3 NOW IS A TREE (NEPHITES & LAMANITES)
DEAD BRANCH (NEPHITES)
WHEN THEY CAME TO THE LAST TREE THEY SAW THAT THE WILD FRUIT HAD TAKEN OVER THE ENTIRE TREE AND THE ONE BRANCH THAT HAD ONCE BORN GOOD FRUIT HAD WITHERED AND DIED.
SYMBOLS AND THEIR MEANING
DEAD BRANCH: The Nephites are destroyed by the Lamanites in 385 A.D. Only unbelieving Lamanites remain in the Promised Land.
THE LORD OF THE VINEYARD WEPT.
WHAT MORE COULD I HAVE DONE?
ALL THE OTHER FRUIT IN MY VINEYARD WAS BAD EXCEPT THESE FEW BRANCHES. NOW THEY HAVE BECOME BAD TOO. NOW THE WHOLE VINEYARD IS GOOD FOR NOTHING.
THIS LAST TREE I PLANTED IN GOOD GROUND. IT WAS THE BEST SPOT IN THE ENTIRE VINEYARD.

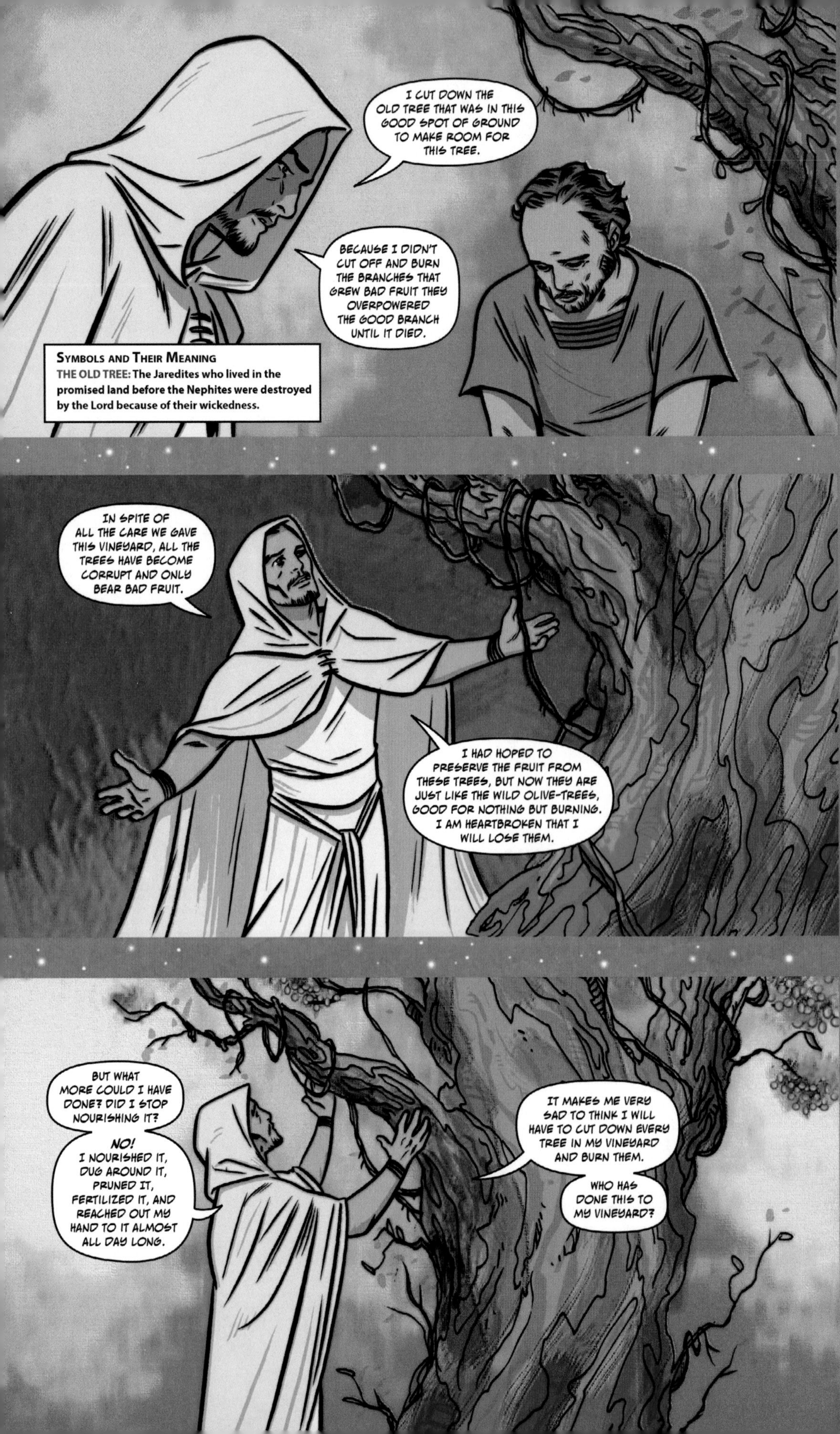
I CUT DOWN THE OLD TREE THAT WAS IN THIS GOOD SPOT OF GROUND TO MAKE ROOM FOR THIS TREE.
BECAUSE I DIDN'T CUT OFF AND BURN THE BRANCHES THAT GREW BAD FRUIT THEY OVERPOWERED THE GOOD BRANCH UNTIL IT DIED.
Symbols and Their Meaning
THE OLD TREE: The Jaredites who lived in the promised land before the Nephites were destroyed by the Lord because of their wickedness.
IN SPITE OF ALL THE CARE WE GAVE THIS VINEYARD, ALL THE TREES HAVE BECOME CORRUPT AND ONLY BEAR BAD FRUIT.
I HAD HOPED TO PRESERVE THE FRUIT FROM THESE TREES, BUT NOW THEY ARE JUST LIKE THE WILD OLIVE-TREES, GOOD FOR NOTHING BUT BURNING. I AM HEARTBROKEN THAT I WILL LOSE THEM.
BUT WHAT MORE COULD I HAVE DONE? DID I STOP NOURISHING IT?
NO! I NOURISHED IT, DUG AROUND IT, PRUNED IT, FERTILIZED IT, AND REACHED OUT MY HAND TO IT ALMOST ALL DAY LONG.
IT MAKES ME VERY SAD TO THINK I WILL HAVE TO CUT DOWN EVERY TREE IN MY VINEYARD AND BURN THEM.
WHO HAS DONE THIS TO MY VINEYARD?

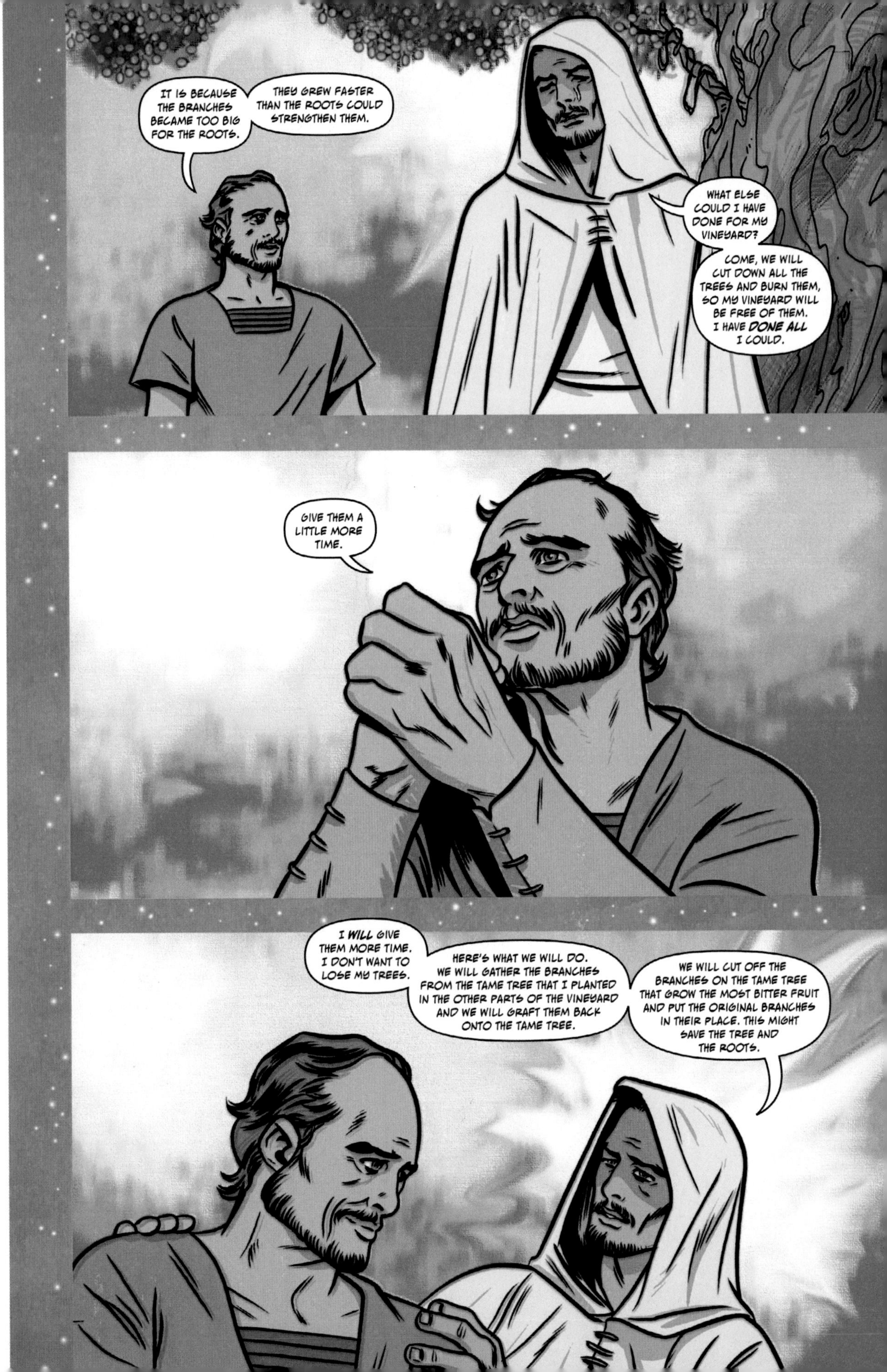
IT IS BECAUSE THE BRANCHES BECAME TOO BIG FOR THE ROOTS.
THEY GREW FASTER THAN THE ROOTS COULD STRENGTHEN THEM.
WHAT ELSE COULD I HAVE DONE FOR MY VINEYARD?
COME, WE WILL CUT DOWN ALL THE TREES AND BURN THEM, SO MY VINEYARD WILL BE FREE OF THEM. I HAVE DONE ALL I COULD.
GIVE THEM A LITTLE MORE TIME.
I WILL GIVE THEM MORE TIME. I DON'T WANT TO LOSE MY TREES.
HERE'S WHAT WE WILL DO. WE WILL GATHER THE BRANCHES FROM THE TAME TREE THAT I PLANTED IN THE OTHER PARTS OF THE VINEYARD AND WE WILL GRAFT THEM BACK ONTO THE TAME TREE.
WE WILL CUT OFF THE BRANCHES ON THE TAME TREE THAT GROW THE MOST BITTER FRUIT AND PUT THE ORIGINAL BRANCHES IN THEIR PLACE. THIS MIGHT SAVE THE TREE AND THE ROOTS.

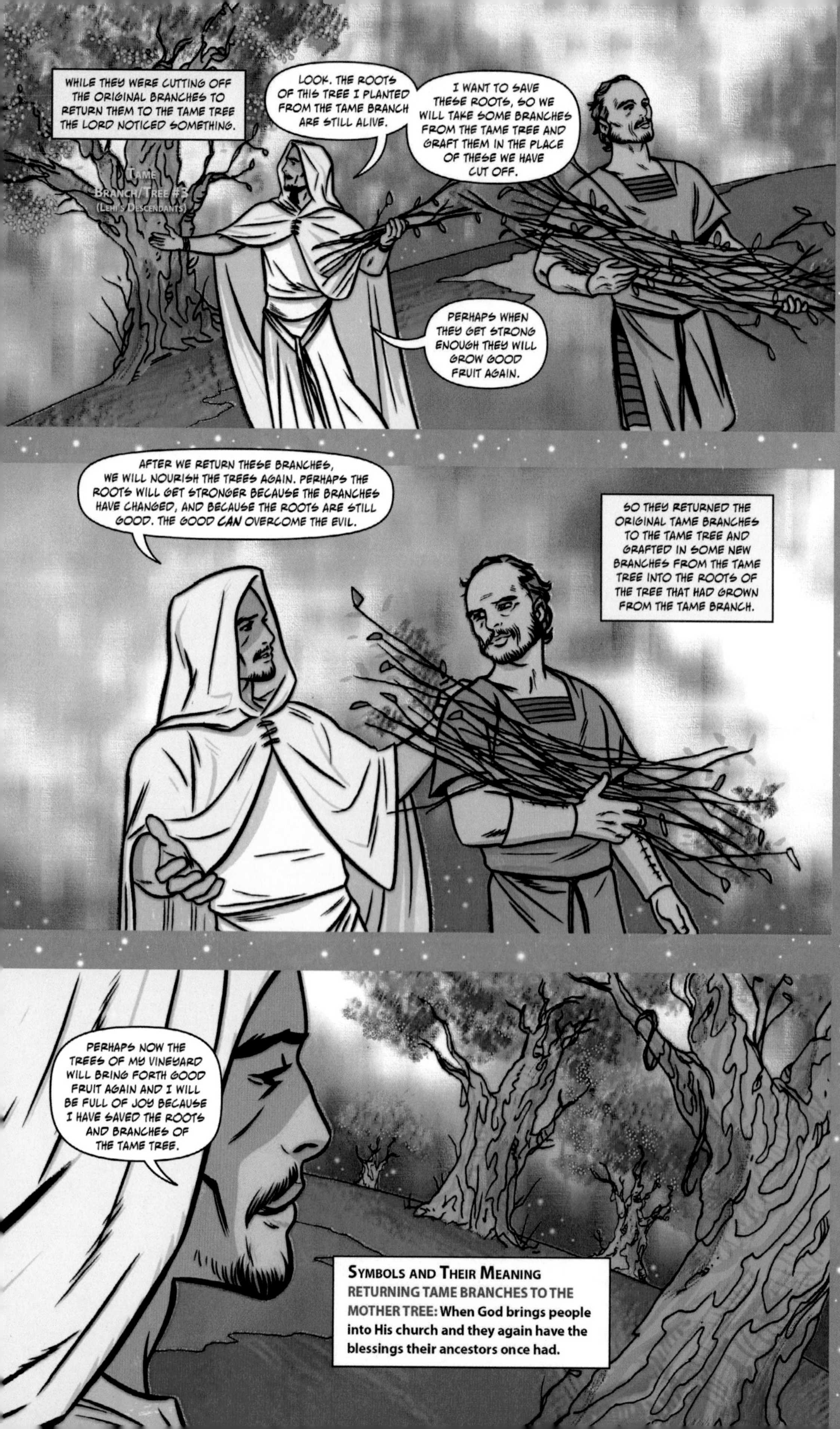
WHILE THEY WERE CUTTING OFF THE ORIGINAL BRANCHES TO RETURN THEM TO THE TAME TREE THE LORD NOTICED SOMETHING.
TAME BRANCH/TREE #3 (LEHI'S DESCENDANTS)
LOOK. THE ROOTS OF THIS TREE I PLANTED FROM THE TAME BRANCH ARE STILL ALIVE.
I WANT TO SAVE THESE ROOTS, SO WE WILL TAKE SOME BRANCHES FROM THE TAME TREE AND GRAFT THEM IN THE PLACE OF THESE WE HAVE CUT OFF.
PERHAPS WHEN THEY GET STRONG ENOUGH THEY WILL GROW GOOD FRUIT AGAIN.
AFTER WE RETURN THESE BRANCHES, WE WILL NOURISH THE TREES AGAIN. PERHAPS THE ROOTS WILL GET STRONGER BECAUSE THE BRANCHES HAVE CHANGED, AND BECAUSE THE ROOTS ARE STILL GOOD. THE GOOD CAN OVERCOME THE EVIL.
SO THEY RETURNED THE ORIGINAL TAME BRANCHES TO THE TAME TREE AND GRAFTED IN SOME NEW BRANCHES FROM THE TAME TREE INTO THE ROOTS OF THE TREE THAT HAD GROWN FROM THE TAME BRANCH.
PERHAPS NOW THE TREES OF MY VINEYARD WILL BRING FORTH GOOD FRUIT AGAIN AND I WILL BE FULL OF JOY BECAUSE I HAVE SAVED THE ROOTS AND BRANCHES OF THE TAME TREE.
SYMBOLS AND THEIR MEANING
RETURNING TAME BRANCHES TO THE MOTHER TREE: When God brings people into His church and they again have the blessings their ancestors once had.

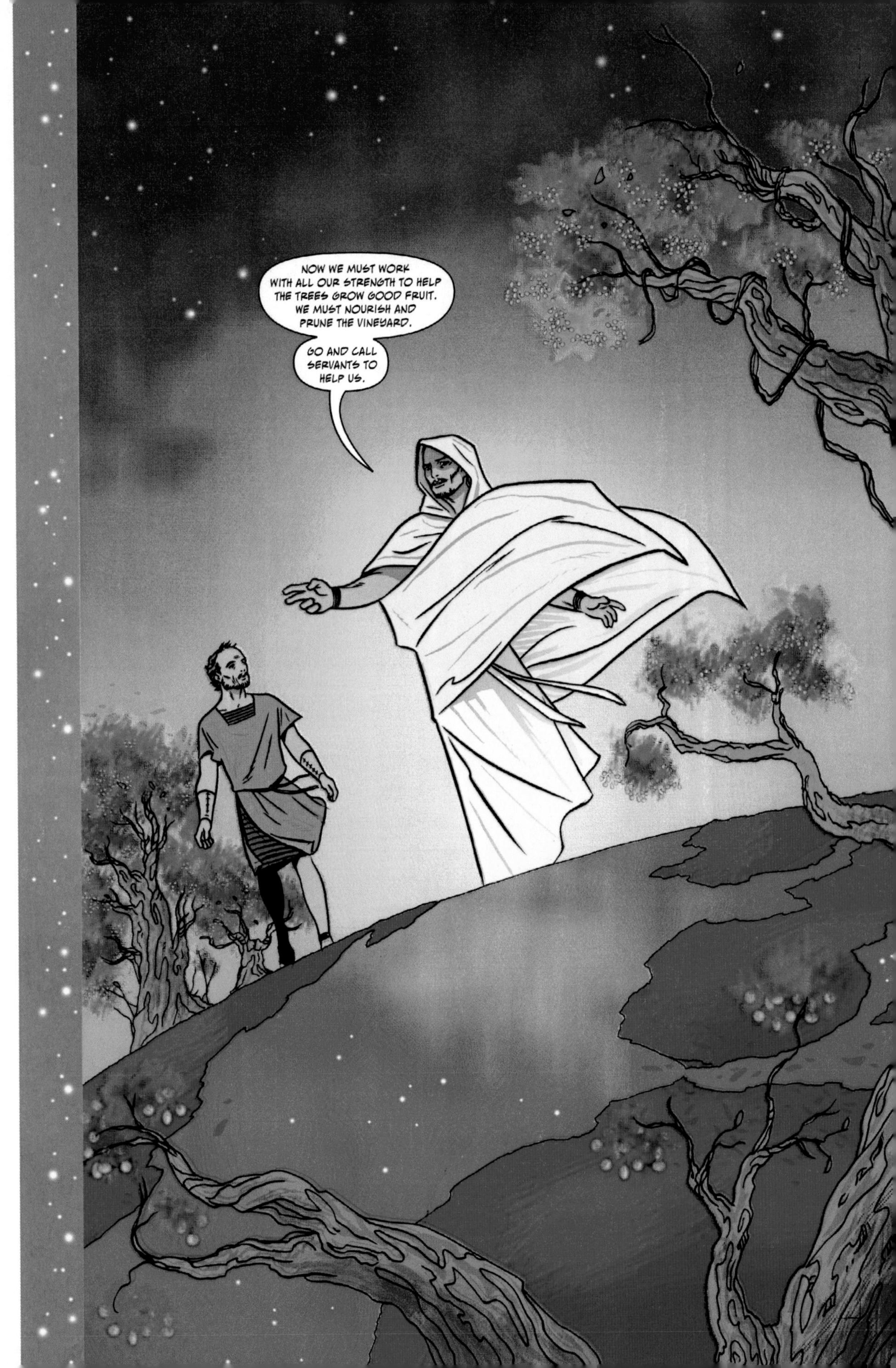
NOW WE MUST WORK WITH ALL OUR STRENGTH TO HELP THE TREES GROW GOOD FRUIT. WE MUST NOURISH AND PRUNE THE VINEYARD.
GO AND CALL SERVANTS TO HELP US.

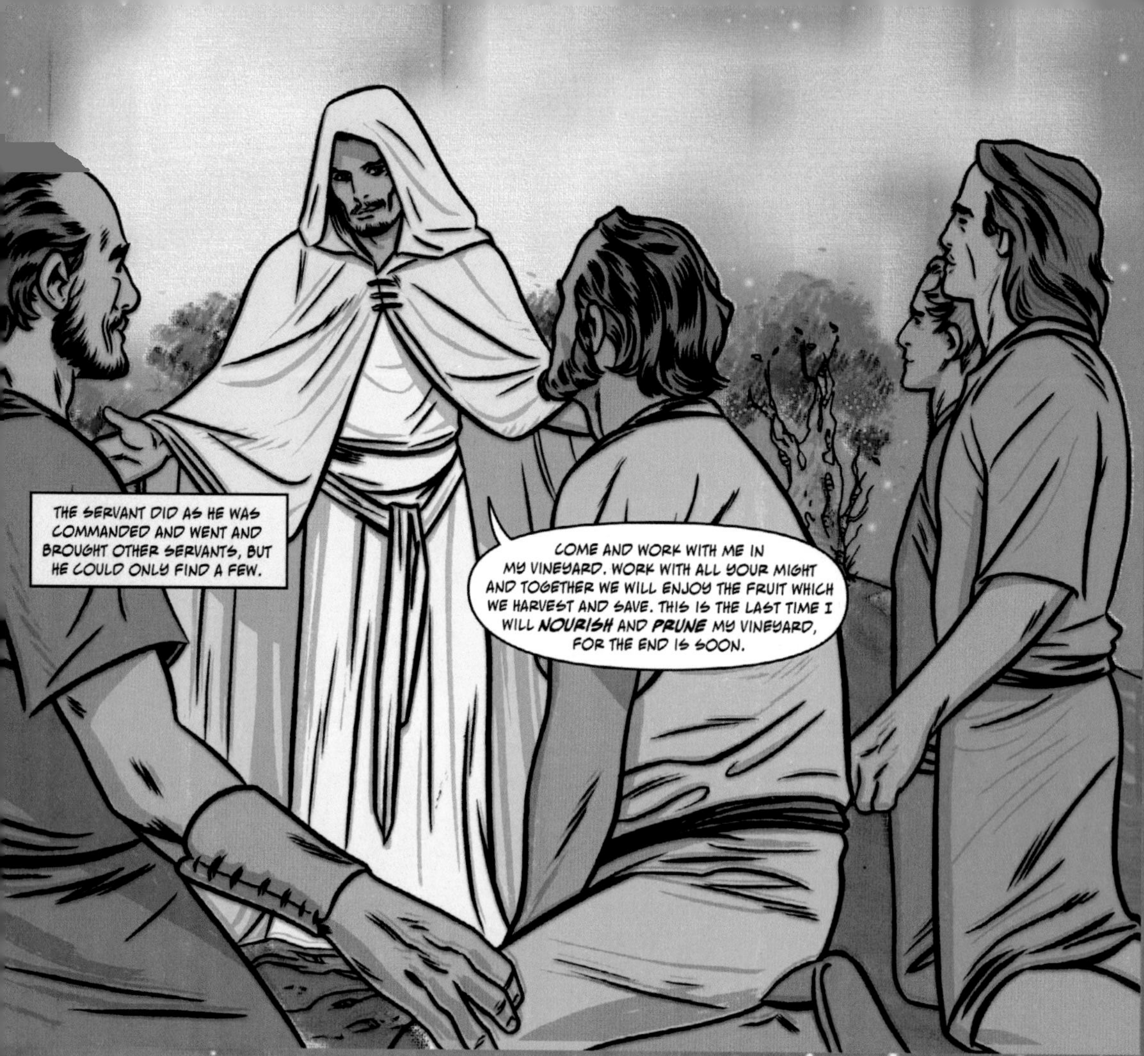
THE SERVANT DID AS HE WAS COMMANDED AND WENT AND BROUGHT OTHER SERVANTS, BUT HE COULD ONLY FIND A FEW.
COME AND WORK WITH ME IN MY VINEYARD. WORK WITH ALL YOUR MIGHT AND TOGETHER WE WILL ENJOY THE FRUIT WHICH WE HARVEST AND SAVE. THIS IS THE LAST TIME I WILL NOURISH AND PRUNE MY VINEYARD, FOR THE END IS SOON.

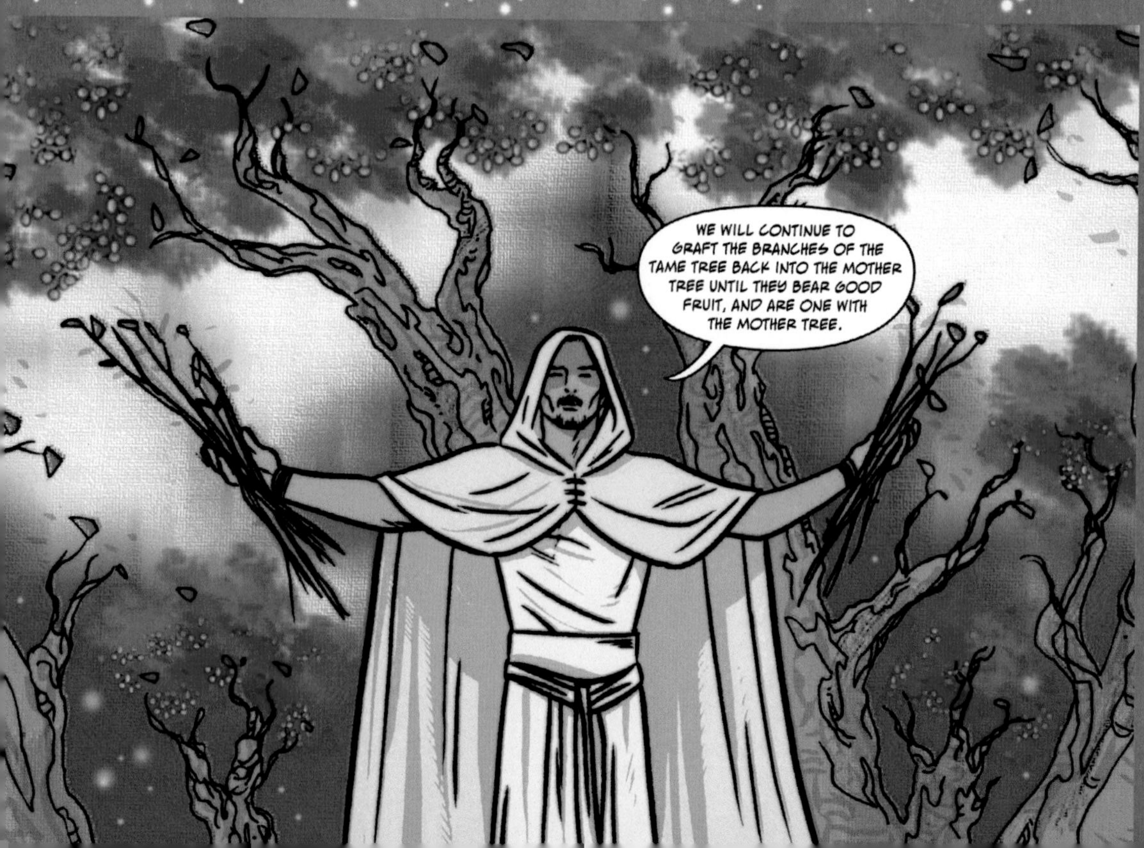
WE WILL CONTINUE TO GRAFT THE BRANCHES OF THE TAME TREE BACK INTO THE MOTHER TREE UNTIL THEY BEAR GOOD FRUIT, AND ARE ONE WITH THE MOTHER TREE.

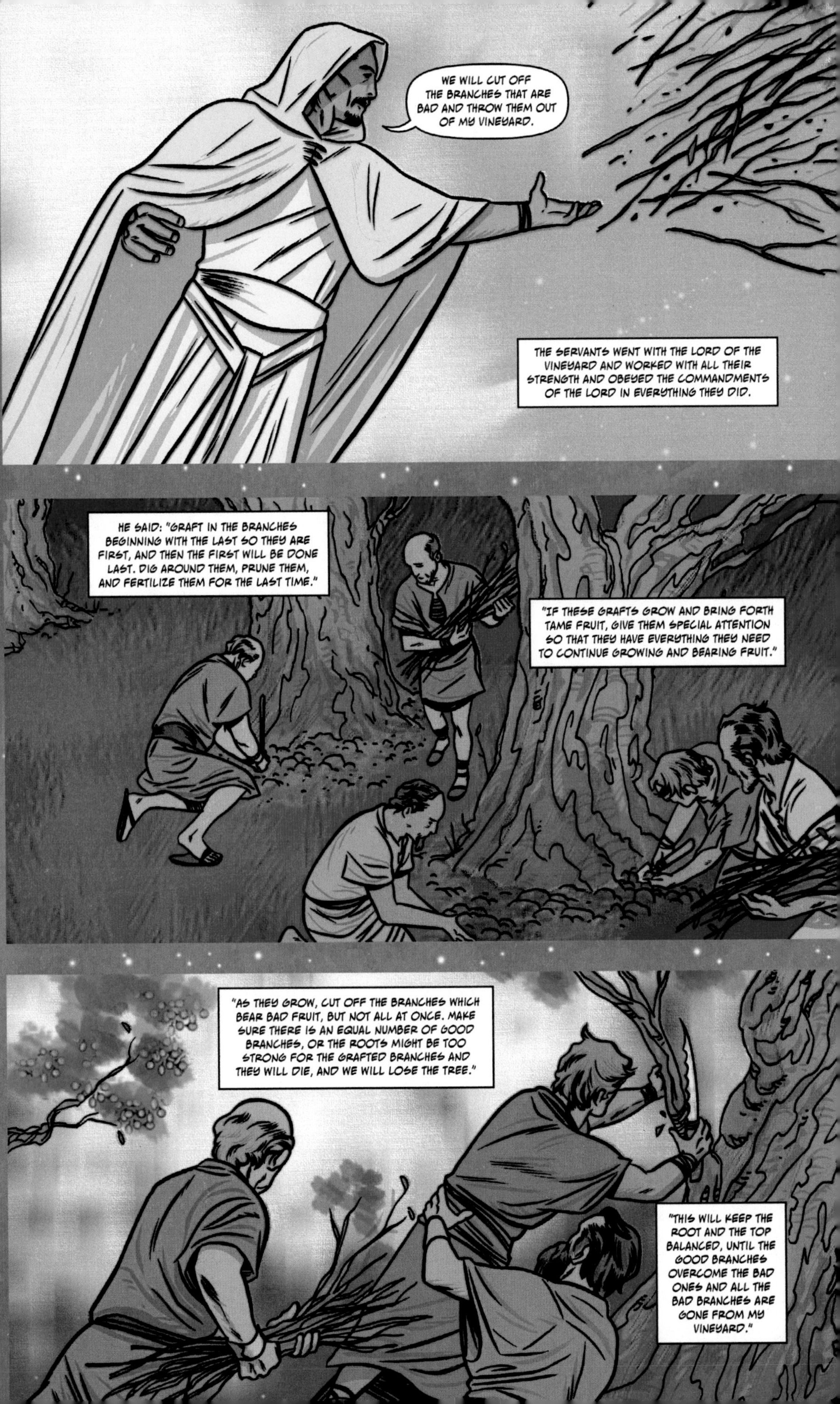
WE WILL CUT OFF THE BRANCHES THAT ARE BAD AND THROW THEM OUT OF MY VINEYARD.
THE SERVANTS WENT WITH THE LORD OF THE VINEYARD AND WORKED WITH ALL THEIR STRENGTH AND OBEYED THE COMMANDMENTS OF THE LORD IN EVERYTHING THEY DID.
HE SAID: "GRAFT IN THE BRANCHES BEGINNING WITH THE LAST SO THEY ARE FIRST, AND THEN THE FIRST WILL BE DONE LAST. DIG AROUND THEM, PRUNE THEM, AND FERTILIZE THEM FOR THE LAST TIME."
"IF THESE GRAFTS GROW AND BRING FORTH TAME FRUIT, GIVE THEM SPECIAL ATTENTION SO THAT THEY HAVE EVERYTHING THEY NEED TO CONTINUE GROWING AND BEARING FRUIT."
"AS THEY GROW, CUT OFF THE BRANCHES WHICH BEAR BAD FRUIT, BUT NOT ALL AT ONCE. MAKE SURE THERE IS AN EQUAL NUMBER OF GOOD BRANCHES, OR THE ROOTS MIGHT BE TOO STRONG FOR THE GRAFTED BRANCHES AND THEY WILL DIE, AND WE WILL LOSE THE TREE."
"THIS WILL KEEP THE ROOT AND THE TOP BALANCED, UNTIL THE GOOD BRANCHES OVERCOME THE BAD ONES AND ALL THE BAD BRANCHES ARE GONE FROM MY VINEYARD."

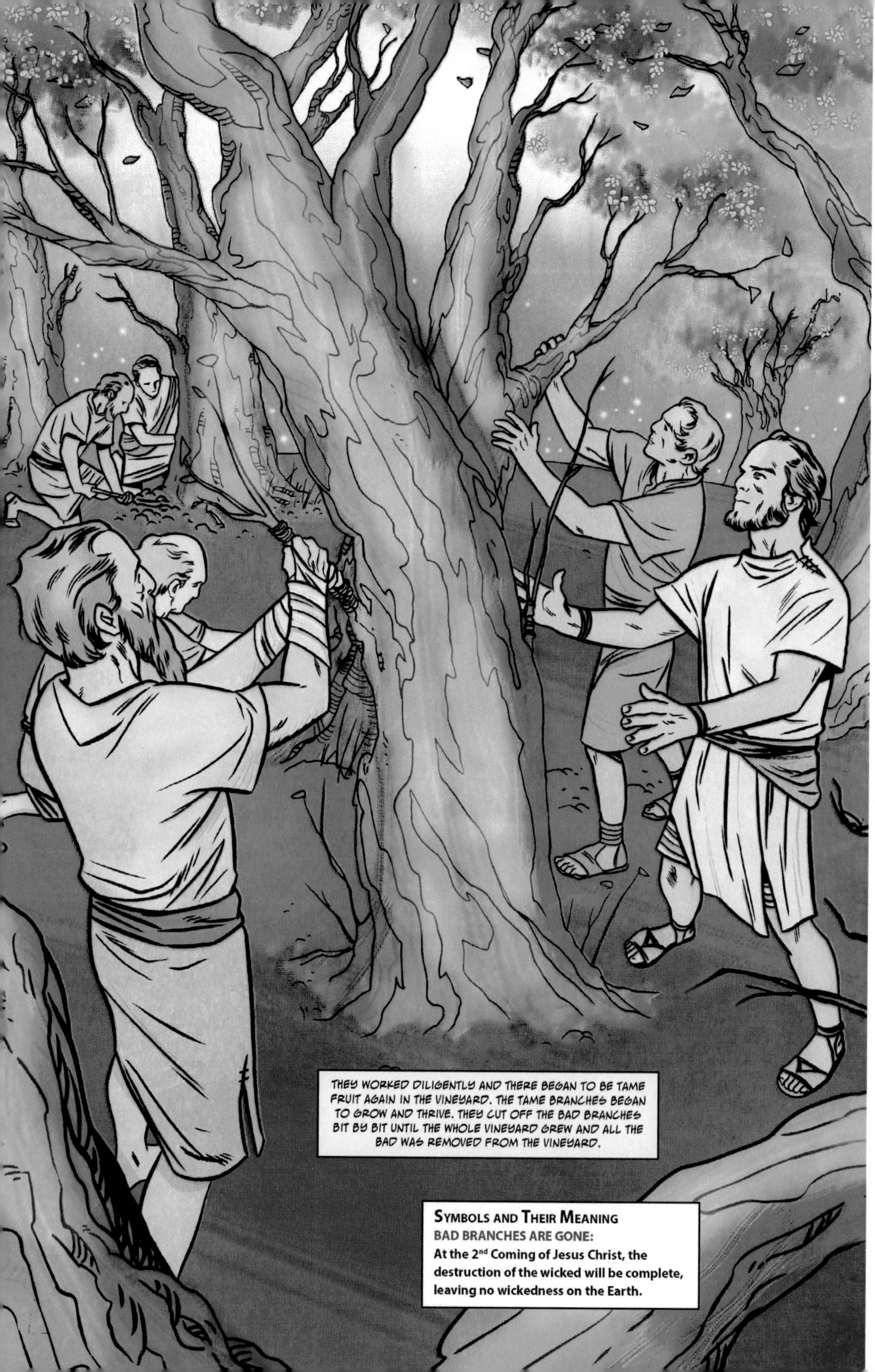
THEY WORKED DILIGENTLY AND THERE BEGAN TO BE TAME FRUIT AGAIN IN THE VINEYARD. THE TAME BRANCHES BEGAN TO GROW AND THRIVE. THEY CUT OFF THE BAD BRANCHES BIT BY BIT UNTIL THE WHOLE VINEYARD GREW AND ALL THE BAD WAS REMOVED FROM THE VINEYARD.
SYMBOLS AND THEIR MEANING
BAD BRANCHES ARE GONE:
At the 2nd Coming of Jesus Christ, the destruction of the wicked will be complete, leaving no wickedness on the Earth.

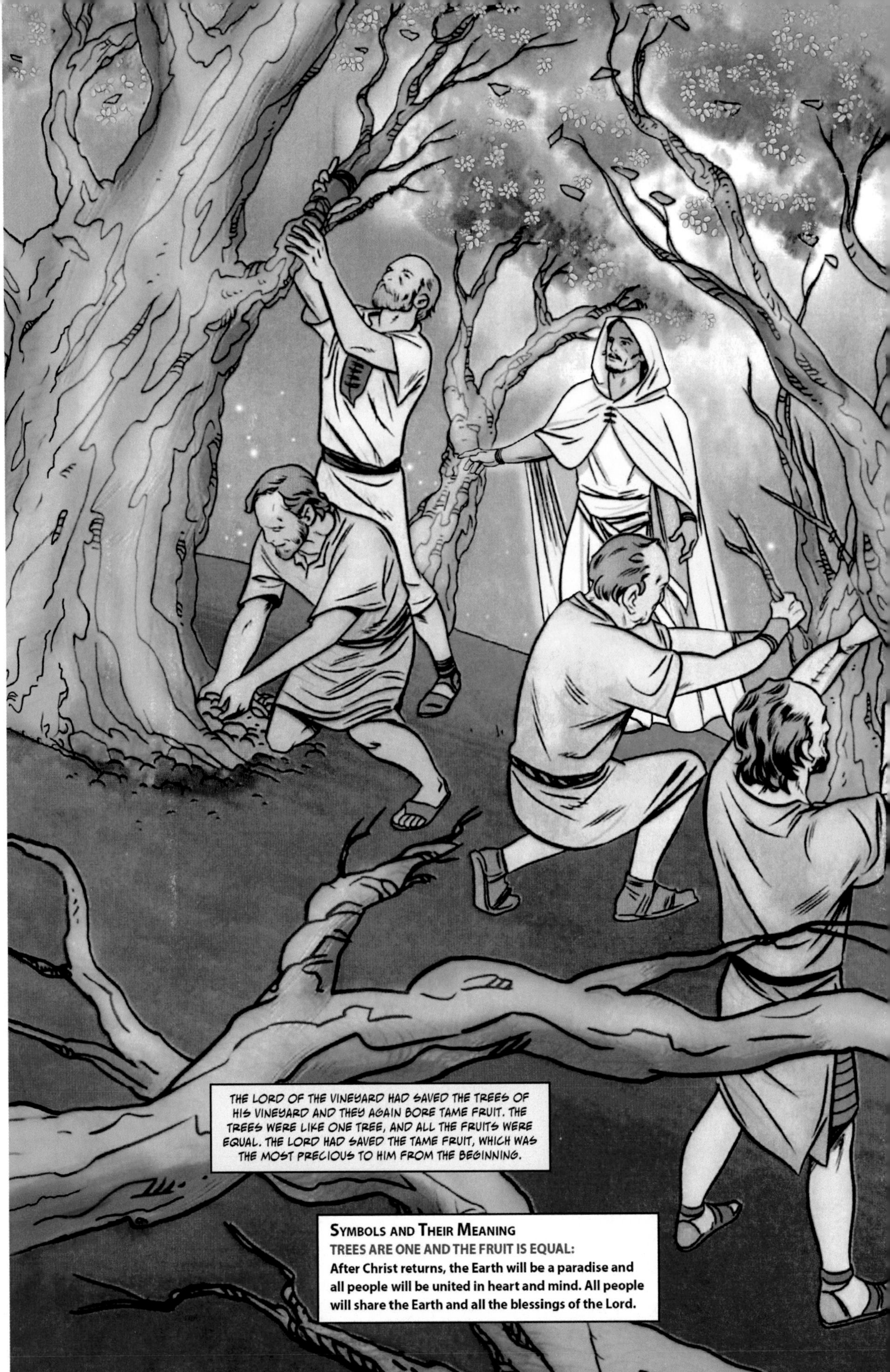
THE LORD OF THE VINEYARD HAD SAVED THE TREES OF HIS VINEYARD AND THEY AGAIN BORE TAME FRUIT. THE TREES WERE LIKE ONE TREE, AND ALL THE FRUITS WERE EQUAL. THE LORD HAD SAVED THE TAME FRUIT, WHICH WAS THE MOST PRECIOUS TO HIM FROM THE BEGINNING.
SYMBOLS AND THEIR MEANING
TREES ARE ONE AND THE FRUIT IS EQUAL:
After Christ returns, the Earth will be a paradise and all people will be united in heart and mind. All people will share the Earth and all the blessings of the Lord.

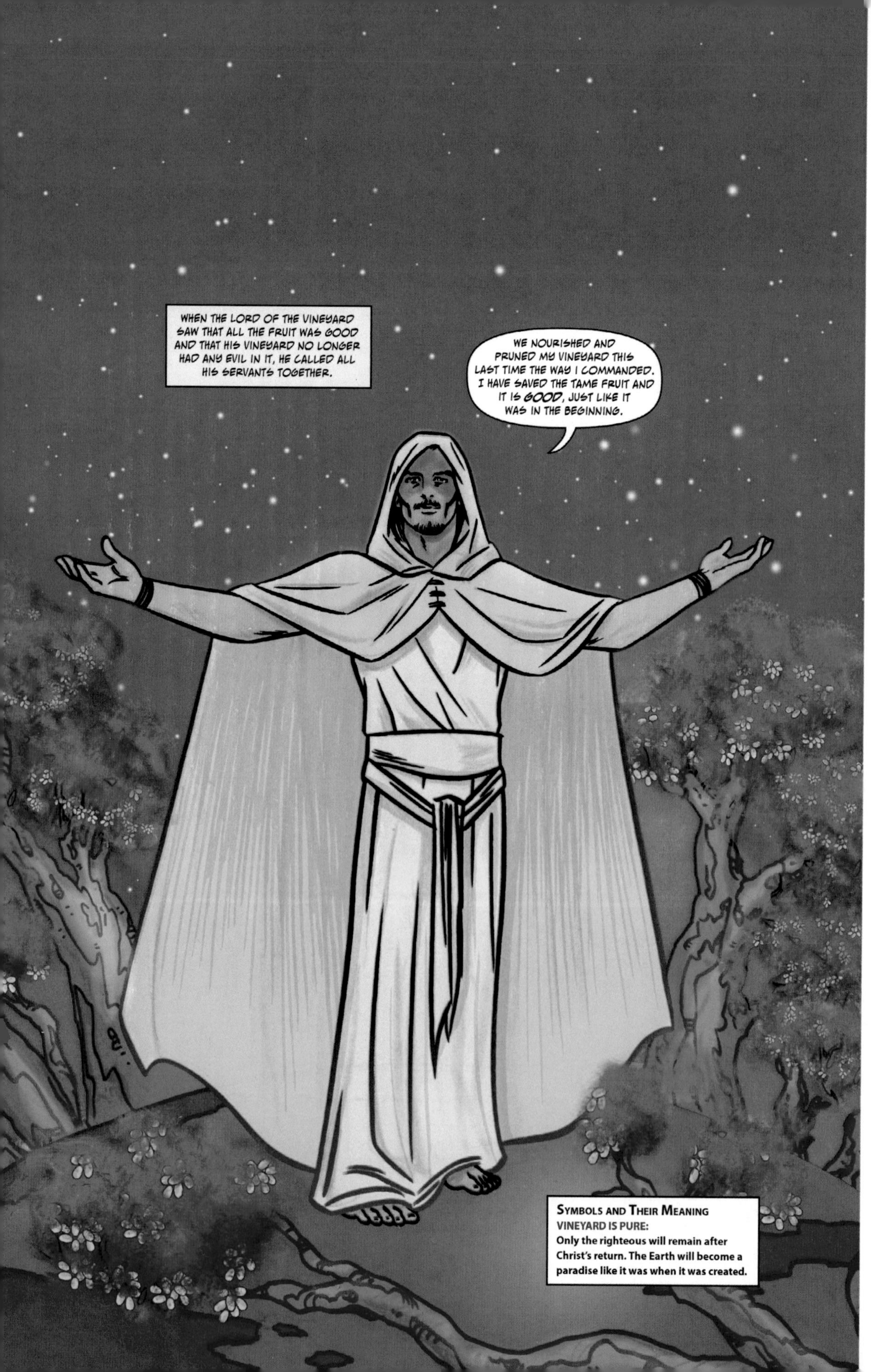
WHEN THE LORD OF THE VINEYARD SAW THAT ALL THE FRUIT WAS GOOD AND THAT HIS VINEYARD NO LONGER HAD ANY EVIL IN IT, HE CALLED ALL HIS SERVANTS TOGETHER.
WE NOURISHED AND PRUNED MY VINEYARD THIS LAST TIME THE WAY I COMMANDED. I HAVE SAVED THE TAME FRUIT AND IT IS *GOOD*, JUST LIKE IT WAS IN THE BEGINNING.
Symbols and Their Meaning
VINEYARD IS PURE:
Only the righteous will remain after Christ's return. The Earth will become a paradise like it was when it was created.

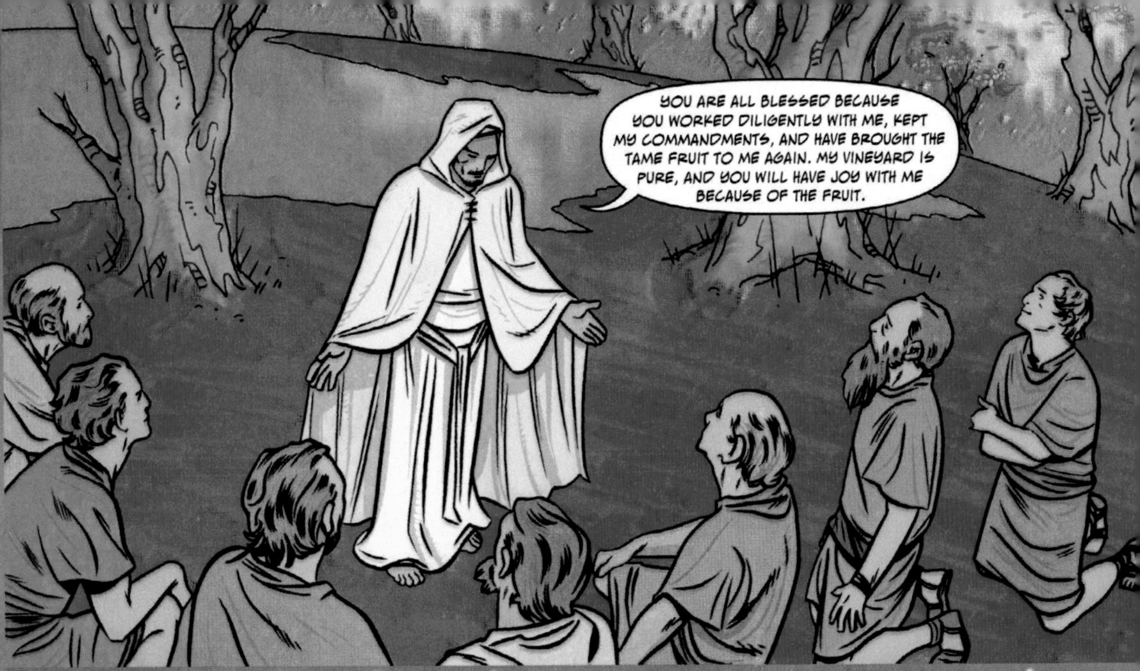
YOU ARE ALL BLESSED BECAUSE YOU WORKED DILIGENTLY WITH ME, KEPT MY COMMANDMENTS, AND HAVE BROUGHT THE TAME FRUIT TO ME AGAIN. MY VINEYARD IS PURE, AND YOU WILL HAVE JOY WITH ME BECAUSE OF THE FRUIT.

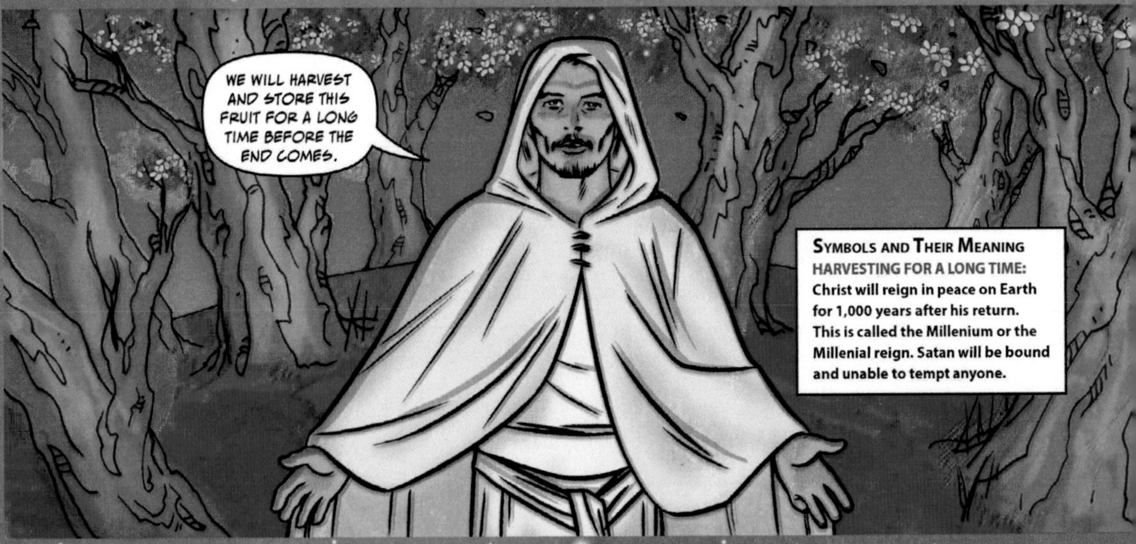
WE WILL HARVEST AND STORE THIS FRUIT FOR A LONG TIME BEFORE THE END COMES.
Symbols and Their Meaning
HARVESTING FOR A LONG TIME:
Christ will reign in peace on Earth for 1,000 years after his return. This is called the Millenium or the Millenial reign. Satan will be bound and unable to tempt anyone.

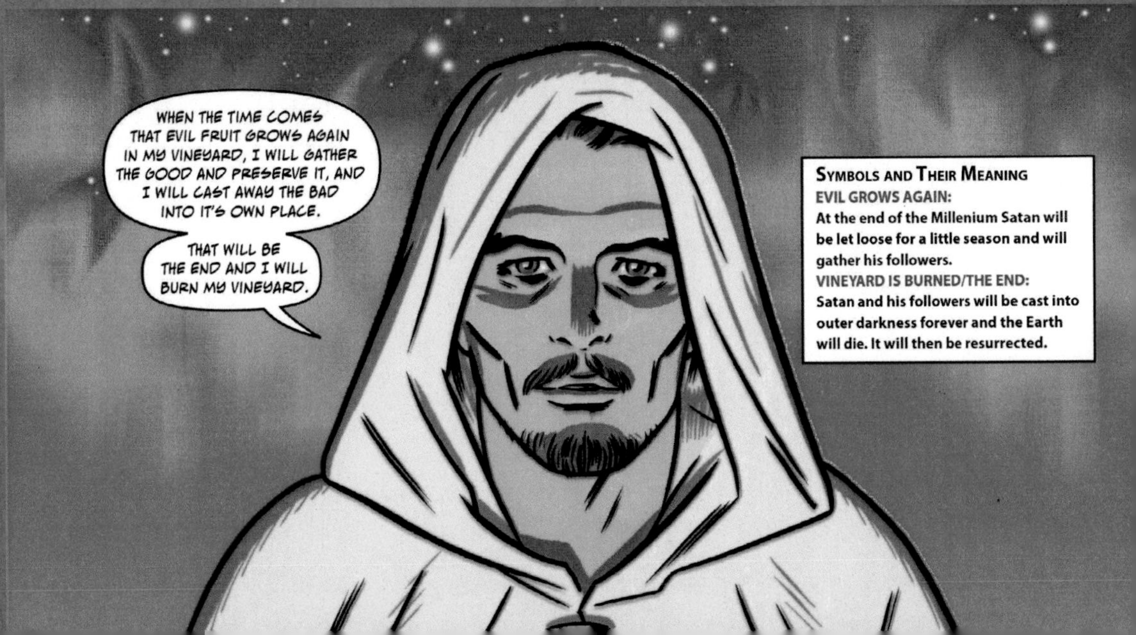
WHEN THE TIME COMES THAT EVIL FRUIT GROWS AGAIN IN MY VINEYARD, I WILL GATHER THE GOOD AND PRESERVE IT, AND I WILL CAST AWAY THE BAD INTO IT'S OWN PLACE.
THAT WILL BE THE END AND I WILL BURN MY VINEYARD.
Symbols and Their Meaning
EVIL GROWS AGAIN:
At the end of the Millenium Satan will be let loose for a little season and will gather his followers.
VINEYARD IS BURNED/THE END:
Satan and his followers will be cast into outer darkness forever and the Earth will die. It will then be resurrected.

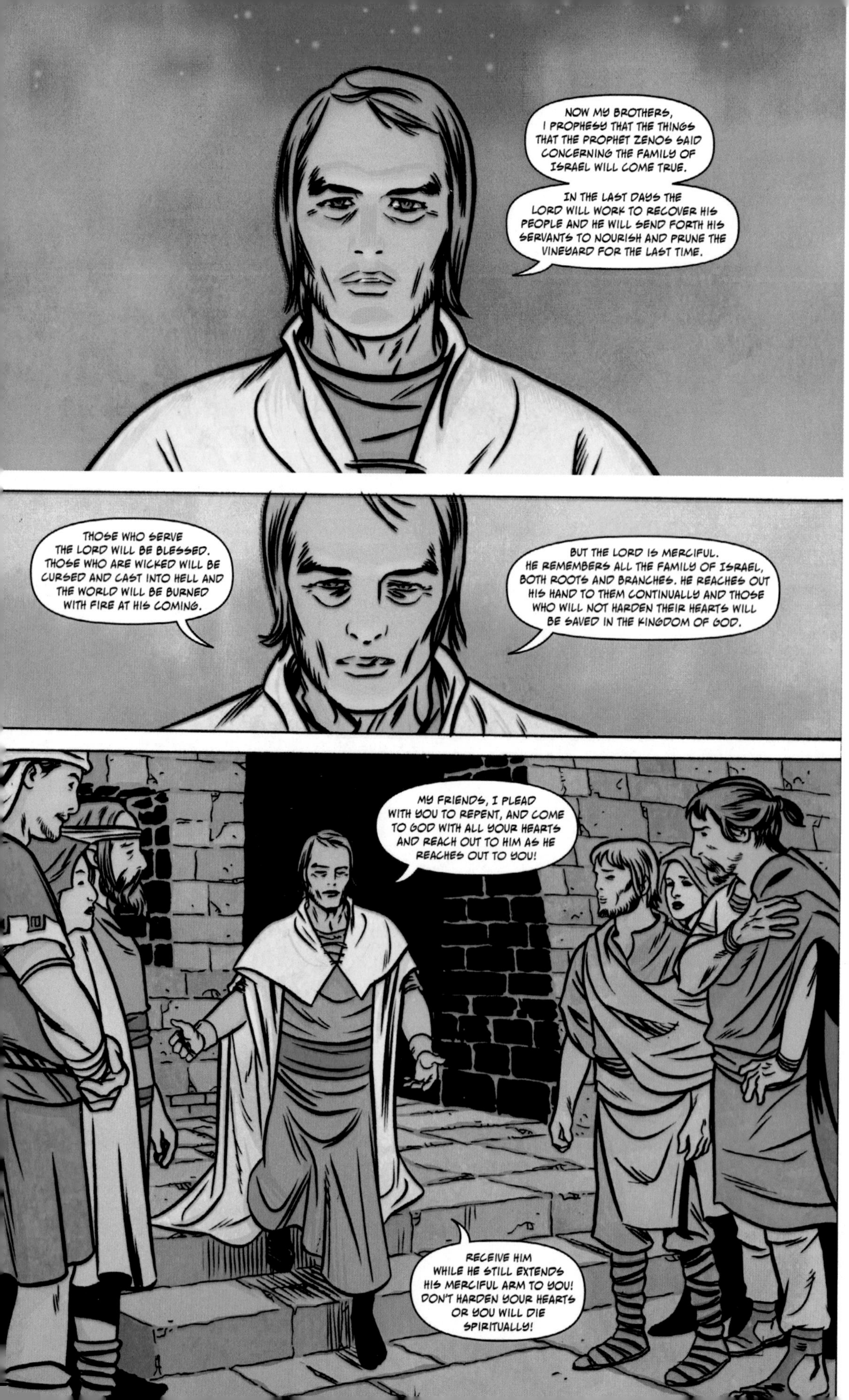
NOW MY BROTHERS, I PROPHESY THAT THE THINGS THAT THE PROPHET ZENOS SAID CONCERNING THE FAMILY OF ISRAEL WILL COME TRUE.
IN THE LAST DAYS THE LORD WILL WORK TO RECOVER HIS PEOPLE AND HE WILL SEND FORTH HIS SERVANTS TO NOURISH AND PRUNE THE VINEYARD FOR THE LAST TIME.
THOSE WHO SERVE THE LORD WILL BE BLESSED. THOSE WHO ARE WICKED WILL BE CURSED AND CAST INTO HELL AND THE WORLD WILL BE BURNED WITH FIRE AT HIS COMING.
BUT THE LORD IS MERCIFUL. HE REMEMBERS ALL THE FAMILY OF ISRAEL, BOTH ROOTS AND BRANCHES. HE REACHES OUT HIS HAND TO THEM CONTINUALLY AND THOSE WHO WILL NOT HARDEN THEIR HEARTS WILL BE SAVED IN THE KINGDOM OF GOD.
MY FRIENDS, I PLEAD WITH YOU TO REPENT, AND COME TO GOD WITH ALL YOUR HEARTS AND REACH OUT TO HIM AS HE REACHES OUT TO YOU!
RECEIVE HIM WHILE HE STILL EXTENDS HIS MERCIFUL ARM TO YOU! DON'T HARDEN YOUR HEARTS OR YOU WILL DIE SPIRITUALLY!

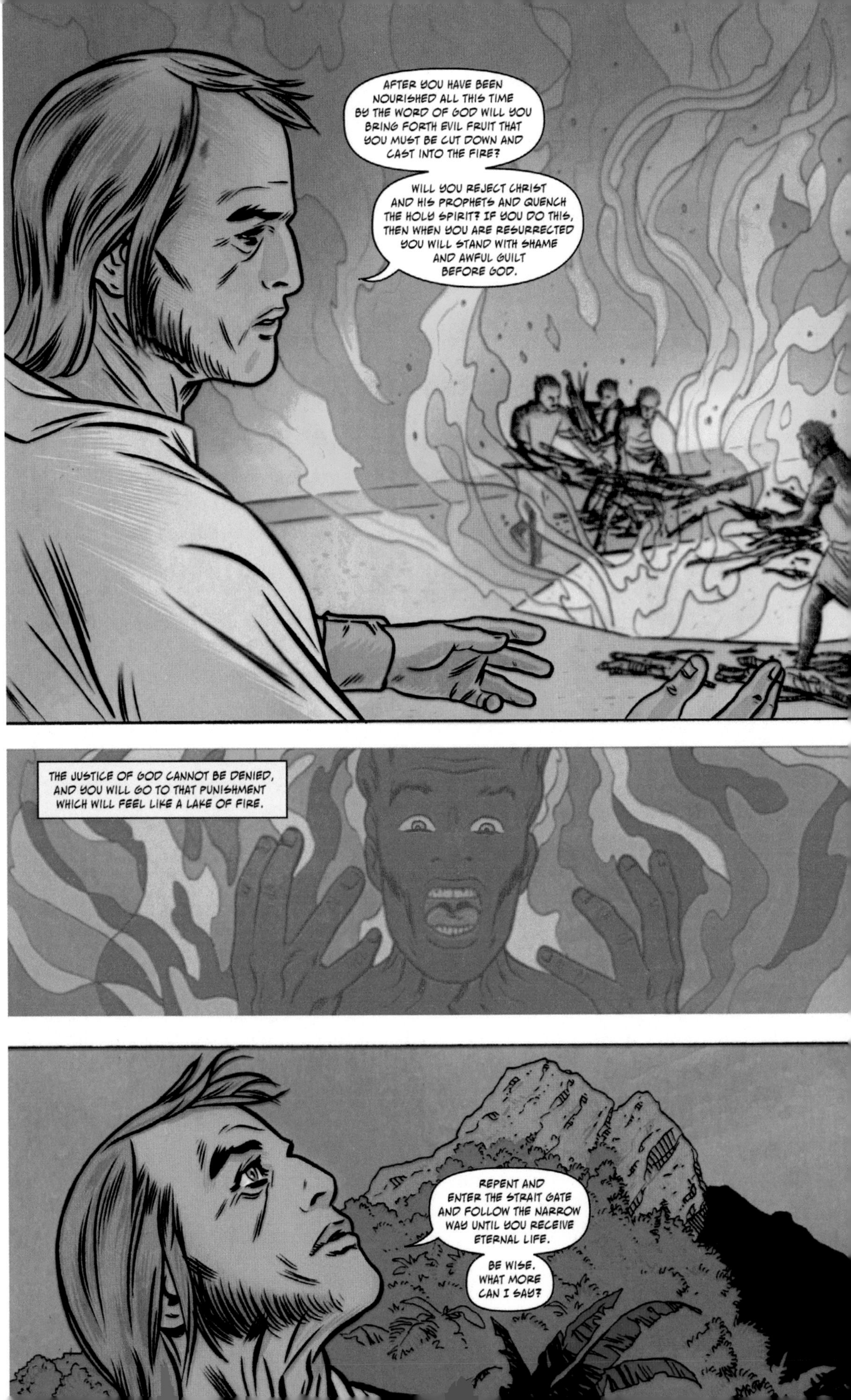
AFTER YOU HAVE BEEN NOURISHED ALL THIS TIME BY THE WORD OF GOD WILL YOU BRING FORTH EVIL FRUIT THAT YOU MUST BE CUT DOWN AND CAST INTO THE FIRE?
WILL YOU REJECT CHRIST AND HIS PROPHETS AND QUENCH THE HOLY SPIRIT? IF YOU DO THIS, THEN WHEN YOU ARE RESURRECTED YOU WILL STAND WITH SHAME AND AWFUL GUILT BEFORE GOD.
THE JUSTICE OF GOD CANNOT BE DENIED, AND YOU WILL GO TO THAT PUNISHMENT WHICH WILL FEEL LIKE A LAKE OF FIRE.
REPENT AND ENTER THE STRAIT GATE AND FOLLOW THE NARROW WAY UNTIL YOU RECEIVE ETERNAL LIFE.
BE WISE. WHAT MORE CAN I SAY?

**If you enjoyed this book and would like to see more created
you can help by:**
Buying or downloading the next volume
Leaving positive reviews
Sharing it on social media
Sending positive feedback to greatldsideas@gmail.com

A MESSAGE FROM MICHAEL ALLRED

The following is an adaptation of the greatest book on the face of the earth, *The Book of Mormon*. Greatest because it holds that key that unlocks all of the mysteries of the universe. It creates a domino effect that leads all that accept it as the truth toward a deep understanding of what all existence is about. There is a purpose in all things. Following the true teachings and doctrine of Christ is the doorway to liberty, joy and the power of creation. It leads to absolute proof that Jesus Christ is in all fact the Son of God, The Savior of the world. He did rise from the grave, a resurrected eternal being of love and light. And it reveals a stunning realization that every life began in a pre-mortal existence and is of infinite worth.

This my testimony. *The Book of Mormon* is a true and inspired record. I know this to be as real and true as I know the world to be round. Every human being can discover this truth for themselves.

Many wonderful and terrible things have transpired in my life–All bringing me to this commitment–the inspiration that led me toward attempting this project. My true intent is to do this work justice–to provide an easily accessible visual thread through all the events in *The Book of Mormon*.

Of course we don't know exactly what these people looked like, and all my research to make this a worthy effort could only ever be insufficient. But I hope it will reach an appreciative and engaged audience just the same. This is a powerful and true generational record that is rich with elements relatable to any soul.

To persuade the reader to the intellectual truth and authenticity of *The Book of Mormon* and to continue my own personal enthusiasm, I'll be including anecdotal and archaeological evidence to peruse.

Most importantly, let me make clear this is in no way a substitute for *The Book of Mormon* itself, which is a sacred book. This project is a primer at best. It is a visual guide, flaws and all, that will hopefully make the events of the actual scriptures come alive and be more easily understood when they are read in full as they should be. The Gospel in it's fullness will be found in the sacred scriptures–not here. But hopefully the spirit will be present in these pages as you, dear reader, turn them.

And so, the following is a 1000-year record of a people who left Jerusalem in approximately 600 B.C. journeying to ancient America where they thrived and battled until their extinction after 400 A.D. They kept permanent records of their history on thin plates of metal, including:

1) The Plates of Brass they brought with them from Jerusalem, consisting of the priceless record of their people, including the five books of Moses and other holy books like Isaiah.

2) The Plates of Nephi (including the Small and Large Plates of Nephi) which were passed from generation to generation from the time they reached the promised land, in the Americas, through the coming of the resurrected Christ (visiting his "other sheep" -see St. John 10:16), to their eventual destruction.

3) The 24 Plates of Ether which contained a history of another people, the Jaredites, who came to the Americas at a time after the fall of the tower of Babel. These records were found in 121 B.C. at which time the Jaredites had been thought to be extinct.

4) And ultimately, The Golden Plates of the Prophet Mormon on which Mormon abridged and condensed all of the above into what is now called known as *The Book of Mormon*. These plates were then sealed up by Mormon's son, Moroni, and hidden under a Stone in the Hill Cumorah until they were delivered to and translated by The Prophet Joseph Smith over 1400 years later in 1830 to begin this final dispensation.

Finally, for anyone who has ever asked themselves the big questions...Does God exist? Who am I? Where did I come from? Where am I going? How can I be truly happy? ...seek out *The Book of Mormon*. Read it. Absorb it. Ponder it. It proves itself to be true. It supports and sustains the truthfulness of the Old and New Testaments, that Jesus is The Christ, and that Prophets live and guide us with love and faith in these latter days. God is always with us.

THE TRUTH OF ALL THINGS

I'm a sceptic and took the long way to what I've come to know to be true. I've always tended to disbelieve everything until the truth knocks me upside the head. So, I'll approach what I write here assuming that I'm addressing sceptics like myself. And, like politics, I completely realize that no one can force their point of view on anyone, and so I will try to be as "matter of fact" as possible.

Where to begin? First off, where did *The Book of Mormon* come from? If it is a work of fiction, it is the most researched, flawless, and prescient work of writing in the history of mankind. If fiction, its author, Joseph Smith, a farm boy from upper New York State, who had a fourth grade education at best, was a genius beyond any measurable level. Many of the archaeological findings that support the authenticity of *The Book of Mormon* as an ancient record were discovered long after Joseph Smith's death. Keep in mind that the Book was first published in 1830. Ask yourself what anyone knew of the ancient cultures of Central America before that time and what of that was Joseph Smith reasonably privy to. From this point of view you begin to build a crushing load of circumstantial evidence that supports that there was no possible way that Joseph Smith authored *The Book of Mormon*. So, if not him, who?

When everything I intend to present here goes back to that question, I ask one simple thing--please keep your mind open to the possibility that God does in fact exist and wants us to have the knowledge that has been shared by prophets and accumulated in scriptures throughout the history of mankind to this day. Big leap? The biggest. Until you take that leap. A leap of faith. Faith and fact. That's what we're dealing with here. And here I'll present facts. And here the reader will determine what those facts add up to. I contend that those facts will support that Joseph Smith was in fact a Prophet of God and did in fact, translate the golden plates of Mormon through the power of God just like he said he did. And for this he was murdered and martyred.

For some of the best detailed cultural and archaeological writings on the subject I would point you in the direction of any of the books by the highly regarded Professor Hugh Nibley as well as *The Book of Mormon on Trial* by J. Milton Rich, *Charting the Book of Mormon* by John W. Welch and J. Gregory Welch, *Light From The Dust* by Scot Facer Proctor and Maurine Jensen Proctor, *Images of Ancient America* by John L. Sorenson, *Land of Promise* by Michael Wilcox, and *Sacred Sites* by Joseph L. Allen, PHD. In the meantime, I'll summarize what has carried the most profound weight for me personally and inspired me toward this project. And keep in mind, though intellectual interest and tangible evidence can prove a thing...feeling a thing is where faith trumps all. Example: Do you have a soul? Can you see it? Faith is a belief in something unseen. In other words, I can only hope that facts will spur a cerebral interest that will result in a spiritual evolution. Without faith, and applying the knowledge, it will ultimately be meaningless. So, take it or leave it. It's up to you.

Exhibit A

The Church Of Jesus Christ of Latter-day Saints. The first American church to actually be named after Jesus Christ. The fastest growing church in the world. According to *U.S. News & World Report*," Since World War II, its ranks have expanded more than 10-fold... more than half outside the United States."

So, is this the true Church of Jesus Christ, restored by the Prophet Joseph Smith in this, the last dispensation of man on earth? It's very clear to anyone who has read this far what my testimony to the answer is. Let's look at the facts.

Joseph Smith and his brother Hyrum were killed in Carthage, Illinois by a mob June 27,1844. The Church and its original members were forced from one community to the next by angry mobs who were threatened by their prosperity, literally running them across the country. These mobs were often formed by local ministers whose careers were at risk by the loss of their congregations to the "Mormon" church (full disclosure: A couple of years ago I found out, after my Aunt Erna Butler gave me an old family journal, that my great great grandfather, Reddick Allred, was one of the early converts and personally knew the first five presidents of the church in his lifetime).

At one point Governor Lilburn W. Boggs of Missouri wrote an extermination order actually making it legal to murder Mormons! At this fragile beginning, in this relatively new nation of liberty, how did the Church survive? How did it actually go beyond survival to actually thrive, even after its leader and prophet was murdered? The American Moses, Brigham Young, succeeded Smith as Prophet and led the greatest pioneer movement in American history. The Church settled and prospered in Utah near the dead water of Salt Lake City where no one gave them favorable odds to last. That city now speaks for itself as one of the most stunningly designed and beautiful cities in America. As Jesus Christ Himself taught in the Sermon on the Mount," Wherefore by their fruits ye shall know them" (St. Matthew 7:20).

I'd like to suggest a book written by W. F. Walker Johanson called *What Is Mormonism All About?* which effectively answers 150 of the most commonly asked questions about The Church and its members. This will leave more space to discuss the book that inspires the virtues.

At the close of this installment I'd like to jump ahead to the end of *The Book of Mormon* where the last Prophet of the book, Moroni, leaves an inspired promise to everyone who reads it and is the key to many conversions: "And when ye shall receive these things, I would exhort you that ye would ask God, the Eternal Father, in the name of Christ, if these things are not true; and if ye shall ask with a sincere heart, with real intent, having faith in Christ, he will manifest the truth of it unto you by the power of the Holy Ghost. And by the power of the Holy Ghost ye may know the truth of all things."(Moroni 10:4-5)

COLLECT ALL 6 EPIC ISSUES!

ALSO AVAILABLE IN DIGITAL FORM
ON AMAZON AND ITUNES

Made in the USA
Las Vegas, NV
06 April 2023

70284043R00026